T0061875

JOE THOMAS:
NOT YOUR AVERAGE JOE

JOE THOMAS:
NOT YOUR AVERAGE JOE

FROM WISCONSIN TO CLEVELAND TO THE HALL OF FAME

MARC BONA AND DAN MURPHY

GRAY & COMPANY, PUBLISHERS
Cleveland

Gray & Company, Publishers
www.grayco.com

ISBN 978-1-59851-128-4
Printed in the United States of America
1

CONTENTS

POSTSCRIPTS

For Lynne.
— M.B.

For Sara, Hayden, McKinley
and in memory of my dad, Jim Murphy.
— D.M.

FOREWORD by ALEX MACK

I didn't know much about Joe Thomas before I was drafted, but after I was selected by Cleveland pretty much everyone had the same response. First, they said, "Congratulations on being drafted." Then, they said, "Wow, you get to be on the offensive line with Joe Thomas. You are going to love him."

They were right.

I knew very little about him actually, just that he was a young player and had made several Pro Bowls already, so he was clearly a great talent. That much was obvious, but then when you get to meet him you see how great of a guy he is. He is a down-to-earth, joyful, gregarious, outgoing, nice dude. He would engage and share his life with the people around him.

I have such gratitude to Joe for being a great teammate and friend. We had a tough stretch of luck in Cleveland, but Joe cultivated an o-line room that was special. He had a way to not take anything too seriously, while taking everything immensely seriously. The culture Joe was a part of making, and one I like to think formed me as a pro, was one where you could have fun and joke around, but also take your job as the upmost important thing. It's a hard line to draw, and Joe did it perfectly.

I owe a lot of my success to Joe. He was such a good role model for how things should be done. He always did the right things, and he was always willing to share all his secrets. We would spend a lot of time between drills talking about the best way to get things done, and the pros and cons of all the different techniques available.

My rookie year during training camp, our o-line coach George Warhop would get on me every day about my hand placement.

He would yell at me and would never really let it go. I would get my blocks done, but he would still yell at me about my hand placement. One day, I was burnt out and tired and I vented to Joe, "Warhop keeps yelling at me about my hands. How come he never yells at you?" Joe, somehow without coming off as smug, matter-of-factly says, "Well, have you ever seen my hands not in the perfect position?" That was eye-opening for me as a rookie. He went on to tell me that I could fix this. That if I focus, I could do this. If you do it perfectly then the coaches can't yell at you for anything. His play on the field was walking proof that you could perfect your craft.

Joe is such a personable and nice guy that this didn't come across like bragging at all. He was just reminding the rookie that coaches have high expectations, but that you should have equally high expectations for yourself as well. It is possible to do it perfectly. You just have to focus because that's what this game requires at this level. Joe expected so much from himself, and that's what made him excellent.

He was so precise on everything he did — foot placement, pass sets, where to punch against any given rush. He knew exactly where to place his hands on every pass set and on every run block. It was a great example for me as a young player to see Joe doing things excellently all the time.

He worked at it, too, every opportunity. I don't think he ever wasted a rep. He had a plan for everything. Every snap. He always had something to work on and would do the necessary work. He would have a game plan every week, every day, every snap. Everything he did had a focus on being the best player possible because he had such high expectations for himself. As a young player, it was great to see that from Joe. To see someone set that bar and see that level of excellence. Because I was his teammate, I was able to see him doing things the right way. That helped me develop really good habits. He had a way to make everything look so simple, smooth and easy. His efficiency was just incredible. He raised everyone's level of expectations.

I spent seven years of my career in Cleveland, and Joe was always there as a role model for how things should be done. As an offensive lineman, you want to be out there for your teammates and Joe embodied that. Your job is to do the best you can to help your team win. He did that. Every snap for his whole career.

Joe had physical gifts to make him a great NFL tackle, but it was his determination and drive to hone his craft, put in the work and strive to be the best he could. He took care of his body the right way, did all the little extra things so he could be out there for his teammates every game, every snap.

He got a lot of credit/recognition and that came with the team not being that good, which is rare. We had a lot of bad Browns teams and we had changeover in ownership, GMs, head coaches and o-line coaches. Through it all though, he always maintained a level of excellence.

There's a perception that if your team is doing well, that it must be filled with great players and that leads to some people being overhyped because they are just in a good scenario. Joe never had that benefit. He was always on teams that ranged from mediocre to struggling. Through all of that, he was still able to gain the respect of players, coaches, teammates and fans. Everyone knew he always performed at a really high level.

The level of excellence he played at was just incredible. To be at that level for that many years is really impressive. His ability to perform at that top-tier level for his entire career is amazing.

Joe is, without a doubt, in the mix of the best left tackles of all time. In this era of football, he absolutely was the best.

That was the football Joe. The regular-life Joe was a fun guy who was great to be around. He would invite you over for dinners. I had many Thanksgivings at the Thomas household. Joe was able to be a great player; that is obvious to the football world. I was lucky enough to see the person Joe was outside of the game, what he meant to his family and friends. He had such a positive influence on my career but also my personal life. I can't describe the sense of honor it was to play with him.

— *Alex Mack, Cleveland Browns center, 2009-2015*

FOREWORD by BRET BIELEMA

"You can't touch him. He's a future first-rounder."

That's what Wisconsin head coach Barry Alvarez told me in 2003 when I asked whether incoming freshman Joe Thomas was going to play offense or defense.

Joe was a legend before I even laid eyes on him.

I met coach Barry Alvarez in Orlando, Florida. I was the co-defensive coordinator at Kansas State, and he reached out to me wanting to know if I'd have any interest in becoming a defensive coordinator at Wisconsin. I started doing some research. That's when I first became aware of Joe.

I remember specifically that first spring, watching him practice and just his effort level, his athleticism. Everything was unbelievable. And I remember I met the track coach early on. I asked him in the middle of spring, "Hey, how good is he at shot and discus?" I was told, "Bret, if he wanted to dedicate himself to that he probably could be a gold medalist in the Olympics in both shot and discus." And that always kind of stuck with me.

I was his head coach for one year. Joe's got three things that are uncharacteristic.

His athleticism for his size is very unique. There's not many people who have his size and power who can bend and run the way he can.

Second thing is he's an incredible perfectionist. There are so many examples, just the detail and precision that he works on in everything he does — not just football, but the way he handles everything financially, everything from A to Z.

And then the third thing that he has, he's just an incredible competitor. A lot of guys will have athleticism and power, but not a lot of them have that competitive nature the way he does, that he just refuses to lose in anything he does.

What I didn't realize, in my first year as a head coach, was that I had a generational player.

I mean, you always have good players. But he truly is, in my opinion, probably the best who's ever played that position in college, for sure. I know there have been a lot of great NFL tackles, but you literally could just take his assignment and count on it. No matter how difficult the assignment was, it was going to be taken care of.

So Joe's last year, I'm a rookie head coach, and I think he's just an incredible player. I witnessed that every game; we were 12-1. And so I reached out to my media person. I said, "Hey, I'd like to call every person who votes for the Outland Trophy."

The response was, "What?"

"I would like to call anybody and everybody who votes on the Outland Trophy to let them know what I think of Joe Thomas, because I want to make sure he wins it."

I literally started calling every Outland Trophy voter, and then when we went to the award ceremony in Orlando, I remember (broadcaster) Chris Fowler came up to me and he said, "Hey, do you want to know or do you not want to know?" And I looked at him. He said, "How's Joe going to handle the moment?" And I remember I told Chris, "I promise you he can handle any moment you throw at him." And it was just one of those things as soon as they announced it, I watched his reaction, and I knew it was coming. And just nothing fazes this young man in any way.

In one game, there was a block about 12, 15 yards downfield. And one of the things that is very frustrating as a coach, you don't mind calls; you just don't like phantom calls. I literally would tell officials before the game, "Hey, if you're gonna throw a flag on 72, you better make sure it's there," because sometimes he puts guys in bad positions just because they're not that good and he's extremely talented. And he likes to finish people. And I say that to the white hat every game.

Well, we're about midway through, and Joe just absolutely took this guy 10 yards down the field, threw him on his back, kept running. I mean, he went in the air. I remember watching it live, and I thought, "Goodness gracious, he just destroyed that guy." And then the flag came out. And I was on this official. "You think you saw something, there was nothing there!" So I was all over this guy's grill.

And then three weeks later, I had the same official in a game. And he came up and said, "I owe you and Joe Thomas an apology. That was as clean a block as I've ever seen." It was really one of those moments.

But the best summary of Joe Thomas is this. We're playing his last game at Camp Randall. It's senior day, and I've seen senior day a million times but never as a head coach, right? And it was a steady crescendo. He was literally the last guy to come out. And so I've said goodbye to two of his high school teammates who were in the same class, and I've shaken everybody's hands, hugging them. I'm kind of emotional. And Joe Thomas comes walking down the ramp, and he is bawling his eyes out. Like I mean emotional times 1,000. And it's a big game, right? We're 10-1 and ranked.

I remember seeing his mom and dad, and they're bawling their eyes out. And I thought, "Holy heck, what's going on here?" Literally gave him a big hug. He ran off to the roar of the crowd. And I remember I said on the headset, "Boys, I don't know what's going to happen, Joe Thomas is pretty emotional." And he went on to play probably one of the most complete games. His ability to flip the switch from professionalism to personal is uncanny.

And that's probably what's made him special.

— *Bret Bielema, University of Illinois football coach;*
University of Wisconsin defensive coordinator, 2004-05;
Wisconsin head coach 2006-12.

JOE THOMAS:
NOT YOUR AVERAGE JOE

PART ONE

GROWING UP

1

GONE FISHIN'

It was a crisp Wisconsin spring day, with temperatures around 50 degrees and steadily rising as Dan Fox's charter fishing vessel Foxy Lady chugged out of Port Washington, about 25 miles north of Milwaukee. It was a day made for fishermen. A list of the fish found in that part of Lake Michigan reads like the menu at a fine seafood restaurant: King salmon, Coho salmon, brown trout, lake trout, rainbow trout . . .

All Joe Thomas wanted was for this day to be as normal as possible.

It wouldn't be. He had a lot on his mind. It was April 28, 2007, and Thomas was hours away from finding out which NFL team would draft him.

He got up around 5 a.m. to head for the dock, arriving to see the sun rise on the lake. Saturday morning fishing was a tradition, but this would be more important than the countless other trips he had taken with his dad. He would soon be leaving his Wisconsin home, but he didn't yet know where he was going. The trip served as a welcome distraction. All Thomas wanted was to spend time on the water with family and friends. Aboard were Eric Thomas, Joe's father; Greg Nelson, Joe's future father-in-law; and Joe Panos, a close pal, mentor and former NFL offensive lineman who had helped coach Thomas in high school.

Dressed in sweatpants, a white long-sleeve University of Wisconsin shirt and red-and-white Under Armour cap, Thomas took in the day. As they boarded, he glanced at Nelson. The realization that he would be marrying Nelson's daughter, Annie, his college sweetheart, sank in. The wedding would be July 7 in Madison. He was more nervous about that than the draft.

"That is when I should be wearing a suit, not now," he thought. This day would be "just a regular day out on the boat."

They pushed off about 6 a.m. and headed in search of salmon, even though it was a bit early in the season. They kept up with the draft coverage via satellite radio, but Thomas tried not to pay attention. They started fishing about 7:30 a.m. It was a bit slow. They caught a few, then traveled farther out for better fishing. Out of cellphone range — even though Thomas was expecting the most important call of his life.

Thomas was under orders — a compromise with the NFL — to be within cellphone range when the draft started at noon. Also, an NFL Network video crew was aboard, although they were not filming live.

They caught a few brown trout, a good omen. Panos hauled in the day's biggest, a 14-pounder. "For where we were," Thomas said, "that was an enormous fish."

The contrast between this setting and the one about 900 miles to the east was stark. There, in Radio City Music Hall in New York City, thousands of people, mostly men, were assembled under one roof in a raucous convention.

Overweight men in the audience, their bellies stuffed into ill-fitting jerseys, screamed in agreement or howled in opposition to announcements coming from the stage. The closer to the stage the more formal the attire ran. Five men in particular looked as if they were part of a fashion show: JaMarcus Russell, his 6-foot 6-inch frame sporting an all-black assemblage. The 6-5 Calvin Johnson wore a thin blue- and beige-striped dark suit, looking like a high-powered banker. Gaines Adams stood tall in magenta tie, dark suit, fancy watch and black cufflinks. Adrian Peterson might have been the most conservatively dressed, in a light blue and gray suit. And Brady Quinn, his body cut more like a fullback than the quarterback he was, squeezed into a brown- and tan-striped suit with an orange paisley tie on a white shirt — usually sans the sports coat with peaked lapels.

At the time, Joe Thomas didn't even own a suit.

To call the NFL draft a spectacle is akin to saying Americans don't mind watching the Super Bowl. Over the years, the draft evolved, thanks to the intersection of an insatiable trio of ingredients: Fan interest, league marketing and media control.

The draft has come a long way since the first one in 1936, when only 24 of 81 players selected chose to actually play professional football. Up until 1980, it was still a relatively modest event. Then, ESPN — a very new ESPN — approached the NFL: What would you think about airing the NFL draft live? Commissioner Pete Rozelle liked the idea. Rozelle took ESPN's request to the 28 NFL owners; they overwhelmingly rejected it. Rozelle exerted veto power and said yes.

"It was a big deal for ESPN because it gave them an association with the National Football League," Fred Gaudelli, who was part of ESPN's draft broadcasts for 22 years, told Sports Illustrated. "By doing the job that we did with the draft back then, it proved to the league that we were real. So when (the NFL) created a cable package in 1987, we were well positioned to get it. That was a big deal for ESPN."

That first televised draft in 1980 was held at the Sheraton in Manhattan, a few blocks from Radio City Music Hall. The Detroit Lions selected Oklahoma running back Billy Sims with the first pick. Cleveland's first selection in that draft was Charles White, a talented running back out of USC who would struggle with drug abuse over his career. The third pick was Anthony Muñoz — like Thomas, a left tackle — by the Cincinnati Bengals.

In 2007, the draft was already the spectacle it has become now, a glitzy show with screaming fans.

Joe Thomas decided he would not be part of that show. That position would endear him to some while irritating others.

"The league was not pleased with my decision," Thomas recalled. "I was one of the first guys to turn down the opportunity. They came back to me multiple times saying, 'You're making a big mistake, we really think you need to go.' They stressed the importance of it — how you can set up marketing deals and make yourself more high profile. If they knew me, they would have known that wasn't a good pitch. I didn't want to be high profile. I am just not a New York kind of guy. That flash just isn't for me."

Also fresh in Thomas' mind was the case of Aaron Rodgers, who had played two seasons at California, completing almost 64 percent of his passes. He had dropped to No. 24 in 2005.

But the league wanted Thomas in New York and it wasn't backing down.

"The NFL tried to convince me to come by saying teams won't want to draft me because I am shunning the draft, that it made me look anti-establishment or whatever," Thomas said. "ESPN and a few other outlets asked if they could join us and do live hits from our boat. Kind of a, 'Hey, look at Joe Thomas out here fishing on draft day,' thing. We thought about it but decided that wasn't what we wanted to do. We didn't want this to turn into a big thing."

According to Thomas, his agent Peter Shaffer initially assumed it was a "foregone conclusion" he would be in New York for the draft. But Thomas let him know he was uncomfortable with that, and that he preferred to go fishing with his dad. According to Thomas, Shaffer agreed.

But the league saw it differently, even reaching out to Bret Bielema, Thomas' college coach, to see if he could persuade Thomas to attend the draft. Bielema had no idea about the push Thomas was getting. After speaking to his former player, Bielema called the league.

"Yeah," he said, "that's not gonna happen."

In the end, Shaffer handled it, but small concessions were made. They allowed cameras on the boat.

"We made it very clear that we didn't want it to be a live draft party sort of thing," Thomas said. "We just wanted to have a good time ... They really did a good job of staying out of our way and just letting us go about our business in the morning."

In the end, it became a good memory, and one Thomas is asked about even today.

That small defiant act itself resonated positively with folks.

How an athlete handles an anticipated, publicized, high-profile spectacle usually won't make or break a reputation, but it can seed opinions in the public's mind. In Cleveland, LeBron James' reputation was tarnished — some would say for a while, others would say permanently — with what became known as "The Decision." That overly hyped announcement in 2010 of where he was going to "take my talents" didn't sit well with Clevelanders who expect just a bit of gratitude for their devotion. But Thomas' decision to fish on a huge day — for him, his family and a new set of fans — was welcomed as a down-home contrast to the glitz of the draft. You would be hard-pressed to find criticism of it. Associated Press columnist Tim Dahlberg lauded Thomas, ending a piece he wrote days before the 2007 draft by writing: "NFL fans are so desperate for football around this time of year, that the ratings will be strong as usual. This year they'll get an added bonus: They can watch a guy fish."

Thomas didn't second-guess himself for his choice of being on the water vs. being in New York.

The night before the draft, Joe Panos had called Thomas. According to an Associated Press story, he said, "I flat out told him, 'I have a feeling Cleveland's going to take you because they need a tackle bad, and I really hope you go at three, because you're perfect for the city, Midwestern guy, blue-collar guy, blue-collar fans, rabid just like the Badgers.'"

In those few words, Panos nailed Cleveland fans.

The next day, out on the water, at 11:42 a.m. Central Time, came what Thomas remembers as "the phone call that would change my life."

Tom Mulhern of the Wisconsin State Journal reported that Thomas heard Browns general manager Phil Savage in the background in discussions regarding him and Notre Dame quarterback Brady Quinn during the six-minute call. When the pick was turned in, Savage told him: It's you.

"I answered the phone, and it was Phil Savage and head coach Romeo Crennel," Thomas recalled years later. "After I reassured them I wasn't in jail or dead, they told me to hang on the line."

"I remember telling them how excited I was and how well I was going to fit in with the Cleveland Browns," Thomas recalls. "Cleveland reminded me a lot of my Milwaukee, a hard-working town. The people of Milwaukee are rabid Packers fans. They live, breathe and die Packers, and that's exactly the sense I got from the people of Cleveland about the Browns."*

He also was excited about who he would be playing alongside on the offensive line. "They recently got Eric Steinbach there, I'll be playing next to him for 10 years or so," Mulhern quoted Thomas as saying.** "It was a cool, fun feeling."

When the Foxy Lady chugged into the marina, about 50 fans and reporters were there. Panos had hooked the day's largest fish, that 14-pound brown trout. Thomas signed autographs.

"They wanted to know what we caught so I held up two fish," Thomas recalls. "The media took some now famous photos and I inadvertently got credit for catching Joe's fish. That's the only time in my life I posed with a fish that wasn't really mine."

Thomas went home to pack for the trip to his new home city, and while he was packing he kept tabs on the draft and saw Quinn was still available. He hoped the Browns would trade up to grab him. Four years earlier, while in high school, Thomas and Quinn had played in the U.S. Army All-American game together. Thomas's hope would be fulfilled.

Browns owner Randy Lerner flew out with his jet to bring Thomas to Cleveland. "Brady Quinn was on that flight and he still had a suit on," Thomas said.

---

* Thomas grew up a Packers fan and was able to watch them on television. The family did not have cable growing up but could see Green Bay play on network television.

** Steinbach would have an eight-year NFL career, playing four years with Cincinnati and then four with Cleveland. His last year was 2010. But he and Thomas are linked in another way: Both had beers named in their honor by Cleveland-based Great Lakes Brewing Co., the first craft brewery in Ohio. The brewery once made the wonderfully named "The Stein Bock" and then years later crafted 73 Kolsch.

A couple of weeks later, a reporter from a local paper asked Thomas about his life at that point. Thomas admitted he didn't know how big of a deal the draft was to so many people. "Even if I wanted to completely escape," he said, "you just can't do it anymore. It's impossible."

Welcome to the media spotlight.

Reflecting on his decision to eschew the glitz of the draft ceremony for the serenity of the water back home, Thomas said there was another reason besides just wanting to be with his family.

"I didn't like the fact that previous players talked about draft day like it was the pinnacle of their career," he said, "and then they could just kind of put it in cruise control after that moment, like 'I've already been drafted and made the money.' And I kind of thought of it differently, like that's just the beginning, where you find out where the work is going to start. So part of it, too, is like that mentality of this is not the end of my story. This is just the beginning, and it's only up from here."*

That April morning on Lake Michigan, Thomas reeled in one fish. The Browns, though, had caught a bigger one.

---

* Thomas' point is well taken about seeing the draft as a beginning and not an end. While viewed as one of the greatest offensive linemen to come out of Wisconsin, he was not the greatest prospect at his position in Big Ten history. That honor arguably goes to Tony Mandarich, a heralded player who was the No. 2 overall pick in 1989. Of the first five picks in that draft, Mandarich is the only one not in the Pro Football Hall of Fame. He played about half as many games in the NFL as Thomas.

2

CHILDHOOD AND SPORTS

"This will be a gift"

Joseph Hayden Thomas was born Dec. 4, 1984, in Brookfield, Wisconsin, to Sally and Eric Thomas.

On the surface, Thomas was a suburban kid who lived with his parents and two siblings. But he took to sports — all sports — early in life. That's not to say he was a star out of the gate; he wasn't. But sports — competition, athleticism—was in his blood. It was nourished, though not forced, by his parents. An innate desire, ability and willingness to work combined to help fuel Joe Thomas on fields and courts.

He wasn't alone on the journey. Sports and competition became a unifying bond for Thomas and three pals — Luke Homan, Steve Johnson and Ben Strickland. They formed a friendship at a young age — rare, healthy and true.

"We're all kind of different in how we're wired. But we were all wired to be really competitive," Strickland said of the group. None had brothers close in age, and that contributed to the friendship the four had, he said.

"That's what kind of helped us build our bond, we didn't have brothers around the same age as us. So we became brothers."

Everything started in Brookfield.

Brookfield, Wisconsin, is a lot like many cities and towns across the United States. Immigrant settlements, a farming base and nearby rail lines all contributed to its growth over 200 years.

Mostly Swiss and German settlers established roots in the area, and named their town after Brookfield, New York, where some of them had come from.

In the early part of the 1800s, Brookfield, Wisconsin, grew — at least by 19th-century standards. Farming was big — wheat, wool, barley — and butter was churned in huge amounts. Baseball was played as a diversion in the town, with established teams.

Brookfield battled its share of growing pains and challenges. A fire in 1905 caused by an overheated stove ravaged multiple buildings, including a meat market. The town rebuilt.

Two years later, a tornado struck late at night. It blew in windows, damaged barns, and turned smaller wood buildings into toothpicks. It ripped up streets and downed early phone lines. Again, the town came back and has existed as a fairly quiet neighbor of Milwaukee.

Brookfield has had its share of famous residents. Probably the best known is notorious gangster Al Capone, who for a time lived in a 1929 French Eclectic home, reportedly because there was no nearby police department. The home supposedly included an escape tunnel and could accommodate seaplanes landing with smuggled alcohol.

Not all the famous residents were nefarious. Brookfield native Caroline Quiner married Charles Ingalls; the couple's daughter, Laura Ingalls Wilder, would grow up to write the pioneering "Little House on the Prairie" books. Harry and Roy Aitken, born and raised on a Brookfield farm, would leave for the nascent limelight of Hollywood during the burgeoning silent-film era.

Heavy train traffic with multiple lines, more so than in many other Wisconsin communities, contributed to Brookfield's growth. Elmbrook Church, founded in 1958, is one of the largest churches in the United States.

For a city of fewer than 40,000 it is a traveler's haven: It has a dozen hotels and about 1,850 hotel rooms, with highways slicing its southern border. Fiserv, a Fortune 500 financial-data services company, is headquartered in Brookfield and has about 44,000 employees. Its name graces the building and court — the Fiserv Forum — where the Milwaukee Bucks and Marquette Golden Eagles play.

But on an early December day in 1984, as the Green Bay Packers to the north were stumbling along at 6-8 and the Wisconsin Badgers were preparing for the school's sixth bowl game in school history, Joe Thomas was born. He was 22 inches and just under 10 pounds. He was named after a great-grandfather who later died when Thomas was very young. Thomas' mother's family has German ancestral roots. His father was adopted, and his paternal lineage is uncertain. Two siblings — William and Jessica — would come along.

In 1984, the world was going through its usual turmoil. News of the day included the recent aftermath of one of history's deadliest and widespread man-made disasters. Two days earlier, an accident at the Union Carbide pesticide plant in Bhopal, India, resulted in the release of poisonous gases. More than 15,000 people were killed and the surrounding area left contaminated for decades. The vice president-elect of Nicaragua canceled a trip to the United States, insulted and miffed over restrictions from the Reagan administration. The University of Wisconsin was preparing for a visit from Geraldine Ferraro, who was part of the Democratic ticket in the 1984 presidential election, the first female vice presidential candidate representing a major U.S. political party. Daryl Hall and John Oates sang their way to the top of the charts with "Out of Touch." Apple's groundbreaking Macintosh computer, which had come out that year, was nearing its first holiday sales season.

But in Brookfield, Eric and Sally Thomas had a son.

Eric grew up in Whitefish Bay on Lake Michigan a few miles north of Milwaukee. He met Sally, who was from Wauwatosa, during their freshman year at the University of Wisconsin-Eau Claire.

Sally didn't play sports, but Eric did — the same ones their eldest son would play: Football, basketball and track. In football Eric was a punter, defensive lineman and running back.

"We ran a wishbone. And I was the fastest person in the backfield. So I was the pitchback on the wishbone option," he said. He played two years of basketball and four years of track — shot put.

Joe Thomas was, by all accounts, an active kid.

"He had a lot of energy," Sally said. "I would tell him, 'Joseph, I'm trying to make dinner.' He's running around. I would say, 'I'm gonna stand at the kitchen window. I'll count how long it takes you to run around the house, and then I'll call out how many seconds and then you run the second time and try and run faster.' So I would be washing dishes or something. And he'd come back — 'How many minutes? How many seconds?' And I'd have to call it up. Then he'd have to go faster. Oh, my gosh, he was very competitive."

Sally said her son always had to be the one who swam the fastest or ran the longest.

Nick Hamel was one of the first people outside the Thomas family to see that competitive edge and energy. He lived across the street, and met Joe when they were both maybe 5, Hamel remembers. They would play for hours, usually outdoors.

"Basically, anything sports related. We did our share of video games, and just causing havoc in the neighborhood. It got to the point where I was pretty much over there every day. We'd be doing something together. We didn't get into that much trouble."

To Hamel, Eric and Sally were like a second set of parents. "They were fantastic," he said. "She used to make us food all the time. She used to always do the diagonal cut on the sausage sandwiches."

But the two boys were very different in size. Thomas was a big kid while Hamel's frame was on the slight side. So playing together, roughhousing, could be a recipe for injuries.

"The biggest one was he snapped my collarbone as we were playing football against each other," Hamel said. "We would do usually some sort of sports — we learned to play soccer together, we learned to play baseball together. We played football, whatever have you — hockey. So that particular incident, I managed to sneak around him, and he and his big legs caught up to me and unfortunately he landed on top of me which, as a small little kid, that didn't end well."

Hamel was 9 at the time. He doesn't hold a grudge. "It wasn't exactly fun, but it could have been worse."

"We basically taught each other sports. He certainly had more of a natural inclination. A lot of our interactions — at hockey or whatnot — ended up with me somehow breaking a finger or something like that."

Bones weren't the only thing that wound up broken.

Once, when they were about 10, Hamel recalls: "We were sword fighting with a broomstick and a bat. He knocked the broomstick out of my hand, sent it sailing through a window that his mother happened to be in. Then we took off running like kids do when they break a window. Ran around to the front, trying to hide behind this tiny rock, his mom comes down. 'I saw you guys running from the back. What are you doing?' His mom was good at keeping us on task. I mean, she kept us both in check."

But there was a tenderness lurking within the big kid who just wanted to play and win. In middle school Hamel and Thomas were at track practice when an accident happened that showed another side of Thomas.

"I was running hurdles," Hamel said. "We're running on this asphalt-like fake track. Joe was clear on the other side of the track, and I hit a hurdle and face-planted into the asphalt. And when I looked, Joe is the first person sprinting across the track to come get to me, and he reached me before anybody else did who are about 10 feet away. Just that kind of caring personality where he, you know, he's going to get there to make sure you're OK."

It wasn't all broken bones and smashed faces.

Hamel remembers joining the Thomases on trips to their family cottage, about a 30-minute drive away.

"His birthday is in December, but he always celebrated it in July. And we always went up to his cottage to celebrate that. It was an interesting thing to do to get us all together. There'd be some sort of huge water fight. His dad would get super involved. It was always fun. It usually ended up being all the kids versus Eric. He kept us entertained for sure."

The cottage also provided opportunities to teach the kids about water, boating and outdoors life.

The Thomases moved a few blocks away when Joe was in seventh or eighth grade. The distance wasn't far, but it was enough so that he and Hamel didn't keep up their regular play schedule. Joe's interest in sports didn't wane. In fact, it was just beginning.

Joe had another interest, cultivated by his father: Fishing. In the spring, Thomas' father said, they would drag a boat to Door County, Wisconsin, north of Green Bay, and follow the brown trout, which traced the smelt down the shoreline until they hit Milwaukee in May.

"In Wisconsin, you get to have three rods per person," Eric Thomas said. "And all the person has to be able to do to be called a person is to hold a rod. And Joe was a big kid. At 2 or 3, he was able to hold a rod. So I'd bring him along, throw him in the bow of the boat, give him some Ninja Turtles to play with and a couple of blankets, because it's always dark in the morning. And I mean he truly enjoyed it. And we truly enjoyed him enjoying it on the trips."

Joe would become an excellent student in high school and college. But early on, at Hillside Elementary school, the will to play overrode his interest in learning.

Sally recalls in one class, Joe was penalized for using pen and not putting his name on papers. Turns out Joe also was scribbling his work on homework papers as he held them up on the side of the brick school building, rushing through so he could get to recess. The result was sloppy penmanship on a rushed job.

"He hated to do homework and wanted to get down to the fun stuff," Sally said.

As fun as gym class was, there was a time when Joe Thomas didn't excel in physical education, either.

With big feet, he had a tough time getting through ladder skills of the President's Challenge Fitness Awards, and he didn't pass the "sit and reach" portion of the test. That bumped him to the exam's next lowest level.

"He was very upset about that," Sally said.

Another time — a rare time — Thomas' mouth got him into potential hot water. A mile run was staged at school.

"He was shooting off his mouth, 'I'm gonna beat that record,' going on and on," Sally said. "And then the morning of the competition comes, and he says, 'I have a tummy ache, I can't go to school.' And I said, 'You're fine, what is going on?' Then he's crying. 'Oh, I told everyone I was going to beat the record.' I said, 'Well, you shouldn't have shot off your mouth, so off to school you go.' He was not happy, but he came through."

He went to school, and he ran the mile — and he beat the record. But lesson learned: Work hard, keep your mouth closed.*

Virtually no sport was off limits to Thomas. He played everything, from pickup hockey with Nick Hamel to organized soccer on a competitive team. For a while, his parents wondered if he would ever become coordinated.

"The first things he did were baseball and soccer, and in soccer, he was so much bigger (than the other kids)," Eric said. "And the team that he played on had one girl. And she was so much quicker that by the time Joe would raise his leg back to kick, the ball was gone and his leg was coming down. It was going to hit something. And it would, you know, hit other kids." That would prompt cries of 'Get that kid off the field before he kills somebody.' And so you know, as a first-time parent, you're thinking, 'Well, this is going to be my lot in life, I've got a big kid who is never going to get picked for anything, never going to go anywhere. And I'll just have to get used to this.'"

Sally said: "But I also think he grew so fast that he didn't know

---

* When Thomas got to high school, he competed in multiple sports year-round and was in great shape. But his conditioning actually worked against him at one point, his father remembers. For a gym-class test, students had to raise their heart rate to a certain point. Some kids could simply walk at a brisk pace to accomplish that. But Thomas and his pals Luke Homan, Steve Johnson and Ben Strickland — no strangers to sprints in football and basketball — couldn't raise their heart rate enough "even though they were running up and down the stairs as fast as they could go, because they were in great shape," Eric Thomas said. "(Joe) came home saying 'I got a D in gym, I got a D in gym!' He was so mad."

where his head stopped and his feet stopped. And so he would go through these periods of extreme clumsiness and he was always tripping, and he'd bend over and hit his head on the refrigerator door. And it took a while to kind of grow into his body. That was really hard for him. And I remember he must have hurt Nicky or he hurt somebody. And I mean, people don't look well on that. I mean, he's a 10-year-old being a 10-year-old, but he's so big. You don't want your kid hurt by some other kid who's acting like this 10-year-old who outweighs him by 10 or 15 pounds. And I remember him being on the couch in our bedroom just crying because, you know, he had hurt somebody and he had been reprimanded. And Eric told him, 'You know, this will be a gift. I promise your size will be good. But you have a responsibility. You can't act like a 10-year-old when you're going to hurt people.'"

So that was a dichotomy for his parents: It was one thing in soccer to see their son, as a kid, boot a ball the length of the field and have excellent hand-eye coordination. It's another to watch a kid throw a baseball 65 mph and smash into the backstop, forcing parents to cringe, thinking, "Please don't hit him."

"He played youth football, much to my dismay," Sally said. "There was a rule of how many pounds you could be — 140. There was some coach who called him out. And then he had to go into the locker room to be weighed with all of these adults. I mean, he was a young kid, he just wanted to be like every other young kid, and he was just so big that it was really a burden."

His feet, Sally said, were as big then, when he was in sixth or seventh grade, as they are now. "We had a heck of a time finding Rollerblades or ski boots or snow boots when he was in high school. I remember calling the Marquette basketball office because I couldn't find shoes. They were either $400 or they were $10. And he wanted boots, he wanted Rollerblades. He wanted to wear flip-flops. And I'm thinking, 'Where do these people who have kids who have these huge feet buy shoes?' And I told him, 'Can you just ask some of these moms who were there, you know, where they can get flip-flops for their college kid or snow boots?' And bless some mother; I don't even know who it was. She got back and told me to go to this catalog store in Atlanta. I remember when they were outrageously expensive. Now you can get (size) 15, 16, but kids' feet are bigger, but at the time . . ."*

Eventually, Eric and Sally recognized there was a possibility their son might be a decent athlete.

It was when Thomas began playing football in seventh and eighth grade. "You could see some of the athleticism and the size were coming," Eric said. "He's only 140 pounds. But he was playing multiple positions, and nobody could tackle him and he could tackle anybody, could catch up to anybody on the field. It was then that I started to see that, you know, he had some potential certainly for high school."

Some thought he had potential in baseball, too.

Bob Berghaus, a longtime family friend and a sports journalist (now retired), once sauntered over to a baseball game in which Joe was playing when he was 11 or 12. Berghaus had gone to high school with Eric, and his wife and Sally were college roommates. The couples had stayed friendly over the years. Among the small crowd at the ballgame, Berghaus spotted a familiar face from his sports-writing days.

"I saw Kevin Seitzer, who was a member of the Brewers," Berghaus said. "And he says, 'Hey, what are you doing here? You don't have anyone here, do you?' I said, 'No, but I know Joe Thomas.' He said 'Big Joe? He just sent one out of the park. That kid's unbelievable. That kid can do anything he wants.'"**

Berghaus remembered Joe as a polite kid who enjoyed shooting baskets. And he remembered what seemed like a consistent

---

* The difficulty in buying clothes and shoes for a large guy would continue even when Thomas got to college. "He wanted a pair of flip-flops and he went to some place in Madison where they had this big bin of these colored flip-flops," Sally Thomas recalled. "Those old things we used to get for 79 cents? Well, he weighs 300 pounds. After a week they were as thin as paper, but he had flip-flops."

** For the record, when contacted in 2022, Seitzer did not recall the story, though he did play for the Brewers from 1992 to 1996.

growth spurt. Thomas would add a few inches and a few pounds, "but never looking fat or anything like that," Berhaus said. "He just always looked like a young athlete . . . And you just knew, unless he got into trouble — and he was not going to be that type of kid, because of his parents, he was grounded. They're terrific parents. He's who he is because of them."

About this time, the Thomases signed up Joe for a basketball team. "I was a new mom. I didn't know how this works," Sally said. Joe was assigned to a team associated not with his own elementary school. "So he goes, 'I don't want to play' because he wasn't playing with any of his friends," Sally said. "And I said, 'I paid my $15, you are going to play on this team.' I said, 'You never have to touch a basketball ever again, but you wanted to do this. We are committed.'"

Joe kept up the grumbling.

Until they started playing. And winning.

Among his new teammates from that other school were Luke Homan, Steve Johnson and Ben Strickland.

"Luke's dad was the coach," Sally said. Jerry Homan knew something about basketball; he had played college ball at Marquette under the affable Al McGuire. Then came time for the team to play Hillside, Thomas' elementary school.

"Well, they just demolished this other team. And they're playing all these other grade schools and they're winning all these games. And Joe's finding out, 'I like these guys.' And he loved Jerry Homan, Luke's dad."

Sally recalls at the end of the season, Jerry Homan simply asked for the signup fee and said: "We're going to keep these boys together. This team, the Magic, was born. They were playing fourth grade, fifth grade."

They weren't part of the official feeder program that would prepare kids to play in high school. But to the Thomases, that didn't matter.

"They were just having fun," Sally said.

Some parents tried to pressure the Thomases into having Joe

play on an official junior feeder team, even going so far to say he wouldn't get playing time once he got to high school. But Eric saw through the threats for what they were — empty, and silly. Sally recalls he told her, "If a kid has any kind of ability there's no coach who's going to say he's not on my team because he didn't play (on the official team) when he was in sixth grade."

Basketball coach Mark Adams, who coached Thomas in high school, had watched the pals play and saw them come together.

"I saw Joe play. I saw how big he was because, obviously, that stood out for my first impression. But usually the guy who is that big at that age, there is some clumsiness to him. And that wasn't the case with Joe. He was pretty athletic already for a guy his size at that age."

Ben Strickland remembers Joe being a bit gangly for a while, before he grew into his own body. "I think he was about 5-7 as a fourth grader, 5-9, something like that, and obviously still sticking out as far as heightwise compared to other guys. But his ears were probably bigger than his head . . . He was a fawn out there — a big fawn, but he was still working to figure out how his body moved because he was growing faster than he could figure it out."

The growing boys bonded over sports.

"Joe was actually like an all-world type soccer goalie," Strickland recalled. "Brookfield was a big soccer community and always had really talented soccer teams from youth all the way through high school. Joe was on the best soccer team in the state, and he was the goalie. I remember the first time I competed against them. I was on a soccer team, just a ragtag group of guys. And then he was on this select soccer team. Just as a young, you know, fifth grader or sixth grader, I mean, he was a guy who took up the whole goal, just with his wingspan. I remember thinking, 'You can't get anything by this dude.' I think that's where it goes to show, whatever he decided to do and focus on, he was going to be good at it, and he's going to be one of the best at it."

All four of the close friends were solid athletes, and that made a difference. It's one thing for a kid to be good at something; it's another to play a team sport with trusted friends, competing at a high level, where there is an opportunity to form that chemistry coaches and fans love to see. The beneficiary of all this would be Brookfield Central High School.

Brookfield Central is located a couple of miles north of Interstate 94 in an area dotted by churches and the city hall. Brookfield Library is adjacent to the school grounds. When Joe was in school, Central had an enrollment of 1,350. To compare, in 2022, the school had an enrollment of 1,260 but had the feel of a larger school or even a small college campus. Its black-box theater has a professional vibe. The school maintains two basketball courts and extensive athletic fields. In 2022, at least 18 students from the school committed to play sports in college.

Football coaches at Central, including Scott Nelson and Ronn Blaha, were aware of the four incoming freshmen. They knew the boys had been friends for years and they knew how good they were. Not just their athleticism, but also their character. "All four of them on their own were great leaders," Blaha said. "And then you put them together, they made a difference in the whole school. They made a difference on the teams they were part of. It was just a really special thing."

It was at Brookfield Central where Thomas, the kid who didn't like homework in elementary school, would settle into education, showing an inquisitive side to learn. His lifelong respect for the outdoors, rooted with trips to the cottage, would blossom. And it's where he would cement himself as a versatile, talented athlete in three sports.

3

ON THE COURT

Joe Thomas had always played multiple sports. He became best known for football, of course, but as a youth he was also passionate about basketball. And if there was one moment that defined his potential on the court, it came one day in his high school gym.

It wasn't a last-second shot during a big game. It wasn't during a game at all. No media was around, no video.

"A lot of people think Joe was athletic from day one," Eric Thomas said. "From my experience, that was not the case. He was big, but he wasn't necessarily athletic until junior high."

But on this day, this moment would make people take notice.

"The reaction of some kids was horror," Eric Thomas said.

Sally Thomas worked as a nurse at the school. She recalls, "I was finishing up, and one of the kids runs in, 'Mrs. T! Mrs. T! Joseph broke the backboard! Oh my God!' And all I can think of is 'It's a brand-new backboard, oh my gosh, how much is this going to cost me?' They were supposed to be doing some kind of drills or warm-up or something, and they start this crazy dunk contest. It just shattered in a million little pieces everywhere all over the gym."

Thomas had the same reaction as his mother.

"I remember when I broke it I instantly got really scared that first of all, I was in trouble, and second, I was going to have to pay for it," he said. "And those things are not cheap. I'm thinking 'Oh crap, where am I going to have to come up with this money?' Thankfully, they didn't make me pay."

Basketball coach Mark Adams' reaction is why Thomas thought

he had to pay for the backboard. Adams recalls that it was the first time that had happened at the school.

"Everyone could see I was ticked," he said, "because we couldn't go full court anymore that day and until it was fixed," he said.

Adams then turned to Joe, keeping a straight face. "I told Joe 'I don't how this works — it's never happened before, but you might have to pay for it.' He looked like he'd seen a ghost. I waited a few seconds and had to tell him, 'Don't worry about it.' I knew we had another in storage somewhere."

Adam Dahlke, a basketball teammate, remembers Thomas looking imposing early on in high school.

"You come into the gymnasium and here is this guy, 6-foot-6. He really must have been outside a lot this summer — super tan. He was just chiseled. You're like, damn, in high school you just don't see that. It was like if you bought a piece of plywood and stood it up — huge, wide frame, super tall. 'Oh, this is Joe Thomas, the incoming freshman?' Holy smokes."

Adam Ciborowski remembers first meeting Thomas in summer league basketball. "I think he was in eighth grade. And we were kind of poking fun at him. He's a big guy, right — 6-4, 6-5? And I remember poking fun at him by saying he couldn't dunk. And he slam dunked the ball harder than I've ever seen. The ref of the summer league came right up and gave him a technical foul. Here's an eighth grader playing for the varsity. He was pretty embarrassed. But it was kind of funny. It was one of those moments like, 'Wow, this kid's real.'"

Thomas was still growing into his size — and early on that sometimes worked against him.

"When he was younger, even though he had the size as a basketball player, he was almost too nice to push people around," Ronn Blaha, one of his football coaches, said.

Another coach, Scott Nelson, agreed. "Well, he always gets the 'Joe Thomas treatment,' right? We still use that phrase. If you push Joe and do whatever, it's OK. But if Joe retaliates, then he's being a big bully."

Close pal Ben Strickland met Thomas during fourth-grade summer, when a friend's father put together a basketball team called the Rat Pack. They played one tournament together. The following year they formed a different team, called Brookfield Magic. Strickland and Thomas would play basketball and football together at Central, and Strickland would walk on at the University of Wisconsin, where he would be a captain on the football team. Over time, he saw his friend develop into a force on the court.

"We were in the state quarterfinals up at the Kohl Center (in Madison) when I realized how physical Joe could be when he wanted to turn it on," Strickland said. "We ended up beating Fort Atkinson at state.* And the guy who had been guarding Joe had two black eyes, he had Kleenex stuffed up his nose as we were going through the handshake line, and it looked like he had been in a bar fight because he was guarding Joe down on the block. And I don't know if you've heard the story about Joe's bone density. He has the highest record of bone density that they measured with the Cleveland Browns. I think it's all in his elbows, because he would use his elbows in basketball and just destroy guys on the block."

A 2002 account in The Reporter in Fond du Lac described Thomas like this: "At 6-8 and built like a battleship, Thomas is probably the biggest player on the floor most nights."

Family friend Bob Berghaus, a sportswriter at the time who had coached basketball years earlier, saw Thomas play a couple of times. He says the potential was there for Thomas to have succeeded in basketball at higher levels. "If it would have been a sport he liked, a sport he wanted to excel in, again with his work ethic — who knows? Maybe he could have been a small forward if he developed a 15- or 18-foot shot. But he played inside and he rebounded well. He went to state as a freshman and he just doesn't make any mistakes. You know, he was not a big scorer at that time. But he was boxing out and just doing everything you should be

---

* Central defeated Fort Atkinson, 50-38. Thomas had 13 rebounds, including nine on the defensive end. No doubt a few left their marks on his opponents.

doing. You know, there's a couple of seniors who were probably leading the team, and he knew his role. And it wound up being a close game — if I remember right it was like a two-point game that went down to the wire — but he played good defense and then rebounded on offense. . . . It would have been a dream to coach someone like him."

Thomas' high school coach, Mark Adams, said Thomas could have averaged 25 points and 15 rebounds. But "we probably wouldn't have won conference and probably wouldn't have gone to state for those four years in a row, because it would have just been all about him. He didn't average a double-double until his senior year."

When Adams looks back at the teams Thomas played on, it's with a smile and the memory of being surrounded by good coaches and a solid core group of players who could lead. That latter attribute can't be taught. That organic quality contributed to the team going to state every year Thomas was at Central. The diversity of talent on the team, Adams said, "allowed us as coaches to do different things with them that we normally wouldn't maybe be able to do."

The 2002 Brookfield Central team was huge by most high school standards: It had Thomas at 6-8, Adam Dahlke at 6-6, Kyle Mars at 6-5 and five players at 6-3 or taller.

It's not that uncommon for a college to have an athletic 6-8 player weighing 250 to 255 pounds. But in high school?

"You can do a lot of different things with that," Adams said. "So we did a lot of pressing, a lot of half-court trapping, continuous trapping, knowing that if we got burned by it, that he was still sitting back there as a safety valve and protecting the basket. And it allowed us to take chances on defense. . . . He was a game changer. After he graduated, we did have to play a different style."

When Adams looks back, he can chuckle over a few moments in Thomas' hoops career. Central received a lot of media attention then, which Adams says wasn't solicited by the school. "I still say to this day that his grandpa was calling different news outlets because we were getting coverage like you wouldn't believe, that somebody was down there pushing us to the press, because it wasn't certainly something I was doing."

Adams remembers Thomas as humble and coachable. "He respected his coaches. He questioned, but he did it in a way that showed he wanted to learn. He wasn't questioning like, 'Why are we doing this type of thing?' And because we had a rule, 'Hey, there's nothing wrong with asking a question.'"

One time, though, Thomas almost went too far.

The team had lost focus during practice, and Adams felt they weren't taking their upcoming opponent seriously.

"I finally started getting ticked off," Adams recalls. "And I stopped practice. I said, 'Hey, we're not going to be playing the Lutheran Home for the Blind, you know?' It sort of stunned everybody a little bit, not that it was that terrible of a comment. And then there was a pause. And all of a sudden, Joe goes, 'Hey, coach, you got something against Lutherans?' And I said, 'No, absolutely not Joe, because I'm actually one myself, Missouri Synod.' And that just shut him up right away. He didn't know what to come back with. Maybe he wasn't going to come back with anything anyway. But my point was made, and we carried on and things went pretty good."

That moment reflects on both player and coach. Thomas knew when and how much to push, and Adams was mature enough to take it but still maintain control.

"We had a lot of fun, just from the bus rides to and back from the games," Dahlke remembers. "He was always joking around. And intelligent — holy smokes, like intelligent in the classroom. He's brilliant, right? But he's also just smart with people. He knew how to interact with people while carrying on great discussion if you wanted to. He was a leader. And it was never perfect. It was never like 'the Joe Thomas show.'"

Thomas had support from his family for his athletic endeavors.

Sally made delicious pasta for pregame "carbo cram," Dahlke said.

One time, Adams recalled Joe played poorly in a summer-league game near the end of the schedule, right before the Thomas family was set to leave on an annual fishing trip. Adams didn't expect him to show for the final game. But he did. When Adams quizzed Eric about it, Joe's father told him they weren't happy about ending his season on a down note, so they postponed the trip. "I thought that was huge," Adams said, "because I know how tight their family is."

Of course, Adams said, Thomas "played like a monster."

Adams also noticed two qualities about Thomas the athlete.

First, Thomas immersed himself in a sport. His favorite sport was whichever one he was playing. Football in football season. Then — except for the eventual recruiting distractions — "he was all basketball."

Second, Thomas loved his teammates. "He looked out for his teammates. He really cared for them." Adams said. "They knew he cared for them. And I think that contributed — we had great chemistry. He's not the only reason, but he was a big reason because of the way he carried himself, in a very humble way . . . from No. 1 man to No. 15 man, he treated them all the same. And I think his teammates really loved him for that, too. And so did the coaches."

With Thomas, there was no showboating, Adams said. The teams he was on understood it was about the whole and not the parts.

Dahlke noted the same quality. "Everyone knew this guy. He was just built differently. But he never was flamboyant about it, right? It's almost like he's out there to prove to people, 'Hey, I'm gonna hustle as much as the next person does.' And it was just the way he carried himself. It was almost like professional for a high schooler. He was always a workaholic in the weight room. He was a workaholic on the basketball court, hustling."

And on the court, Dahlke saw a player with a "sense of focus."

"Here's this 6-8 guy who obviously is built to play football, but he has twinkle toes, and he's dominating in the lane. You try to shoot a shot over him — good luck."

The competitive spirit extended off the court as well as on it.

Adams recalled a holiday tournament in Sheboygan. Thomas,

a junior, was rooming with teammate Darryl Schnell, a senior captain. They were good friends.

"Because it was an overnighter, I gave them all per diem that the school provided, and I told them, 'When it's out, you've got to spend your own money. Every time we were going out to eat, I do a head count. And I'd say, 'Where's Joe and Darryl?' 'They're sleeping in.' It's breakfast. When we got to the next meal, I'd say, 'Well, where's Joe and Darryl?' Finally — I think it was Strickland, who had a smile on his face. I said, 'OK, what's so funny?' 'Well, they're having a contest to see who can have the most per diem left at the end of the weekend.'"

Another time, Central was traveling to a tournament by bus, and Adams couldn't find Thomas. "Everybody got off," he said. "And you could tell when Joe wasn't there, because he was a head and a half taller than anybody. And so one of the other guys was walking out. I said, 'I didn't see Joe; where is he?' 'Well, he's really sick, coach, he didn't feel good. He's just going to lay across the aisle and the seats, and we'll come get him when it's time to warm up.'" The coaches sweated that out. It was a competitive tournament, and they questioned what they would get out of Thomas.

"He came out and had the game of his life," Adams said.

As a freshman on the varsity team, Thomas knew his place. He knew not to say much. Same went for his sophomore and junior years. The seniors were always leading, Adams said; that was the hierarchy.

"He was just sort of waiting, I think, with his core of guys," Adams said. By the time they were seniors, they led us as a group." But, Adams added, "When Joe spoke, you listened."

But there was another sport Thomas would compete in, and excel at, that would exceed his accomplishments on the court.

4

IN THE CIRCLE

Had Joe Thomas not focused on football, some people think he might have made his way to the Olympics — in track and field.

How did that come about? Joe's father had competed in track and field, so maybe it was partly lineage. Joe's size certainly seemed a good fit for the "throws" events — shot put and discus. In shot put especially, he would compete at a very high level in both high school and college.

Brandon Houle, who attended high school in nearby Oshkosh and competed against Thomas before the two became teammates at Wisconsin, knew him as an intense competitor.

"He's very hyper-focused," Houle said. "On his personal side, he's a pretty funny guy, jokes around a lot, likes to have fun. But when it comes down to competing, it's like everything shuts off and he gets on a whole new level. Especially under pressure."

That trait would one day serve him well in the NFL, where Sunday afternoons feature 70,000 screaming fans, close games and television cameras.

In high school, the senior Houle and junior Thomas were good enough to make it to the Adidas Track Nationals against the best high schoolers in the country. "He actually bested me out there with just a killer throw," Houle recalls. "I think at that time, it was his best throw to date. And he ended up taking sixth place and landed an All-American spot."

A year later, Thomas finished second in the meet with a mark of 64 feet, 10½ inches.

"When it's go time," Houle said, "he's ready to go. And you can tell just by his demeanor — his facial expressions. You just know that he's ready."

Thomas' foray into track and field also included the high jump, which he competed in during his freshman year of high school.

"I jumped until it was starting to cut into my shot put a little bit," Thomas said. "And I told my head coach Mark Pulkownik, 'Look, I know getting some points in the conference meet in high jump is great for the team, but it's really hard to — in the middle of my shot put — go run over and try to do a high jump, clear a bar and then run back and try to focus back on doing the shot put.' I was (clearing) 5-10, maybe 6-foot right around there. I mean, I could score some points. But it was pretty obvious, especially as I was gaining weight, that shot put was the thing and high jump was just sort of holding me back from being a better shot and discus guy. So then we cut that out and then just kind of focused on shot and disc. I actually did hurdles, too. I was a pretty decent hurdler. I enjoyed that until I got beat in a conference meet. Then I was, 'All right, I'm not a hurdler, either.'"

Thomas also briefly tried the hammer throw in college.

"They don't have it in high school in Wisconsin, so it was not until college I was exposed to it," he said. "We screwed around with it. It was fun, and I did one hammer throw in a meet once just to score some points. But it's a lot more technical and I had no background and I already was splitting my time between spring football and that was too much. It's super technical."

Why shot put? You might say it ran in the family. His dad competed in it. His mom's uncle, Bill Cross, was a longtime respected track official in Wisconsin. When Thomas was a senior at Central, he competed at state on a rainy day. All eyes were him to see if he could break records in shot and discus, but it was a special moment for the family, since Cross was there, as well.

Steve Marcelle, who competed in shot put against Thomas while attending Green Bay Preble High School (before going on to compete in track and field at Georgia Tech), has a different connection to Thomas. Marcelle was a sophomore when Thomas was a senior. They met in person for the first time at state. But previously, Marcelle had reached out to Thomas for advice.

"I posted something (to an online forum) to see if he'd respond," Marcelle said. "And he actually did. It was pretty cool. So we went back and forth about what he was doing for lifting and whatnot. That was really helpful for me — not that I wasn't doing a lot of the right things, but just a little bit of tweaking on some things and kind of just knowing how much he was lifting so I could put some goals together. I thought, you know, me being a sophomore and him being a senior at that time, that was pretty cool for him to actually respond because he didn't have to do that. For him to even see it, because I posted on some random Wisconsin sports forum. You know, they didn't have YouTube or Facebook or social media back then. It's kind of crazy. There was nothing. I remember when you had the dial-up internet and you went on there and it took probably an hour to post that and for him it probably took an hour to post back."

Marcelle didn't have high hopes when he was a sophomore at state. But he watched Thomas warm up and chatted with him in the downtime between post-competition and podium — where they both would stand.

"I think I even stole some of his warmup (routine)." Marcelle said. He set a personal record and took second to Thomas.

Other seniors might have just blown off an upstart sophomore from another school. Marcelle found a guy who, with a bushy mop of hair, was "just a nice guy. He's relatively quiet in the sense that he doesn't draw a lot of attention to himself." While Marcelle found Thomas well spoken and very likable, as a competitor, he was "very fierce." He even remembers engaging in "a little cat and mouse" with Thomas in competition, trying to gain an advantage by withholding throws at certain times.

Houle first competed against Thomas when the latter was a high school sophomore. He also saw how good he was — and how much better he could be. "The one thing I remember about Joe, it was funny — he had this kind of big bushy mop on his head. And at that time, he still really hadn't filled out into his full potential. He still looked young, he still had a lot of growing and almost developing to do, which is kind of amazing when you think about the talent that he had and how good he was at that point already. But the thing that I found with Joe is, he's just a nice guy. He's relatively quiet in the sense that he doesn't draw a lot of attention to himself."

But he did draw attention in the shot put circle.

In March 2002 he made the Wisconsin track and field honor roll at 56 feet, 8½ inches — second by 4 and a half feet to Houle. A little more than a month later, with graduation looming, Thomas finished first in a late spring meet with a mark of 63 feet, 6 inches. He also finished second in discus, throwing 178 feet, 7 inches.

It was clear Thomas was doing something all athletes and coaches want to see in any sport — steady improvement. Fans might be excited and frustrated by a team winning, say, eight games in a row, losing six, winning seven, losing seven and so on. But that's an unreliable roller coaster. Incremental improvement, however small, by a team or athlete is more valuable.

Thomas' 63-6 throw wasn't far from Stu Voigt's 66-7 state record set in 1966. It was one of several connections between Thomas and Voigt, one being they both would play in the NFL.*

In June 2003, the Lake Geneva Regional News called Thomas the best shot put and discus thrower in the state. He held top marks

---

* The Wisconsin state shot put record that Thomas eyed was held by Stu Voigt, who has several ties to the Thomas family. After attending high school in Madison, Voigt played football at the University of Wisconsin. Also like Thomas, he had an 11-year career in the NFL with the same team (Minnesota drafted him in 1970 as a tight end). After football, he went into banking — like Eric Thomas. After Sally and Eric married, the couple moved to Minneapolis. Eric played rec-league basketball and recalls: "I got to go up against Stu Voigt. I was a short center. And he's only 6-2 as well (actually 6-1). And I couldn't figure out who this guy was. He looked short, but he was just so well built, and I mean solid — like 250 pounds. Somebody said, 'Yeah, he used to play for the Vikings.' It wasn't until Joe got into track that I realized that Stu Voigt is the same Stu Voigt who held the record that Joe was trying to break at the state meet." Final point: Voigt's 1966 mark of 66 feet, 7 inches, stood for almost 40 years. It was broken in 2005 with a heave of 67-4. It was thrown by Steve Marcelle.

in both events. His throw in discus (185-06) is still etched on the leaderboard at Brookfield Central High School, along with his best mark in shot put, 64 feet, 10½ inches. That throw in discus topped his previous best by more than 7 feet. It also was a light-year away from all other competitors: It beat the field by an astounding 14 feet. (For perspective's sake, the Wisconsin state high school discus record was set in 1993 by Luke Sullivan — 193-03.)

Thomas' accomplishments were good enough to earn him a spot at the Adidas Outdoor Nationals. Houle remembered the competition there as being "absolutely insane." They both placed in the top 10.

The relationship between preparing for football — specifically a lineman position — and shot put is worth noting. As Houle puts it: "It's kind of similar. You're trying to move somebody in a little area. . . . If you're a thrower, you're doing everything you're training for, everything you need for an offensive or defensive lineman. So it's only going to complement what you're going to do in football."

Marcelle also dismissed the notion that throwers didn't run. It wasn't long-distance cardio, but rather "a lot of sprints and agility, speed, like shorts-to-speed work stuff. You need that. If you think about it, you're trying to move like a thrower, you're trying to move a 300-pound body as fast as you can in a 6-and-a-half-foot circle. So you need to have that footwork, speed, explosiveness."

How good Thomas was or could have been raises an interesting what-if scenario: Could Joe Thomas had been an Olympian?

Family friend and longtime sportswriter Bob Berghaus covered state track and described Thomas as "always pushing state records."

"To be honest with you, I think if he had gone into track with the type of work ethic and how athletic he is, I wondered if he would have made the Olympic team . . . Just knowing how he is, he probably would have made that team."

Mark Adams, Thomas' high school basketball coach, also weighed in. "You talk about a guy who got into the technical aspects of shot put and discus. And it would have been shot put that he would have more suited for in the Olympics. But he studied the sports. I happen to have shared an office with the guy who was his shot and disc coach, and saw the two of those guys together — I mean, that made him a better coach, too, because he wanted to do whatever he could to give Joe the best opportunity to be successful in track, too. They broke it down about as fine as I have seen anybody do in a high school setting."

When it came to track and field, Houle had the rare position of seeing Thomas from two vantages: First as a competitor, then as a teammate. For him it came down to one thing holding back Thomas from an Olympic podium: Time. "The one thing that I'll say about Joe is I never count him out. He will always find a way to attain what he's looking to do. And I would agree that doing two sports in college is an insane amount of time. And while you have guys who are not in football and just focusing on track, like myself, I can spend all that extra time focusing on my craft and trying to get better. He doesn't have that luxury. And so I do think that had he focused just purely on track, I don't think there's any doubt in my mind that he would have been an Olympian and eventually gotten a medal. I think that he had the talent and he had the drive, and he had the skills to definitely do it."

He also had aspirations.

"I loved shot put. I loved the idea of you competing against yourself," Thomas said. "And I love team sports, too. But just the idea of instant feedback on your performance and your preparation and all the things that goes into it. With track and field, it's a number or a distance. And I liked that side of things. And I was obviously a pretty good shot putter, really enjoyed it. If football didn't divert me, I definitely would have put more effort and attention in shot put and discus. And I did have dreams, because I love the Olympics. I still do. I love the pageantry, I love the competition. And that was something I definitely would have attempted to pursue. . . . For a 19-year-old, who was doing it as a hobby, I felt like, had I committed to it, and committed to gaining the strength and the knowledge of the technique that I needed to. If I didn't have football, in a way, I felt like I would have had a decent shot, at least."

The hypothetical what-if is worth considering. A high school shot weighs 12 pounds vs. 16 in college and the Olympics. Thomas was 23 when the 2008 Beijing Olympics took place. Tomasz Majewski, a ponytail-wearing Polish thrower who wildly contorted himself in the circle, heaved the shot 70 feet, 6½ inches — a personal best in what was viewed as a strong field, and enough for a gold medal.

As a sophomore at Wisconsin, Thomas set the school indoor record in shot put, 62 feet and ¼ inch. The day he set it, his folks were in the stands with Sally's parents. Sally remembers it clearly.

"(Wisconsin coach Ed) Nuttycombe was across the stadium. And we're sitting there watching, and I mean, we'd watched him throw enough. But he launched that thing. And he knew — *he knew* — he threw really far. He just starts jumping and screaming. You can see Nuttycombe across the way, and before the thing landed he's screaming and screaming. And Joseph busts out of the ring and runs up and he's jumping and hugging. Then the numbers came up, and he is really jumping and crying."

Eric added: "It landed past the circles that they had laid out and bounced into the bleachers. So it didn't take a rocket scientist to see that it was a heck of a throw."

Thomas didn't decide to end his shot put career; his body made that decision for him. He spent his junior year of college rehabilitating an injured knee. Later he was busy preparing for the NFL draft. So football's gain was shot put's loss.

5

ON THE GRIDIRON

When Joe Thomas first stepped onto a high school football field, no one was predicting an NFL career. But teammates could see an attitude, a healthy one, that belied his age.

"He was mature," said Adam Ciborowski, a senior on the football team at Brookfield Central High School when Thomas was a freshman. "He was a little more reserved. He was always very inquisitive . . . asking questions of the other guys, in a good way."

At 6-3, 140 pounds, Thomas was like "a little puppy," as Central head coach Rick Synold later recalled in a 2006 Badger Herald article.

But Thomas quickly gained weight and soon had his coming-of-age moment on the gridiron.

When one of Central's senior players got hurt during a game, Joe replaced him. "He played as a true freshman, and he held his own," Ciborowski said. "I mean, I would have gotten smoked if it was me.* Physically, he was there. He probably lacked a little bit of aggressiveness, but also he's 13 or 14 years old. He held his own."

Thomas' close pals Steve Johnson and Ben Strickland also played on the varsity team as freshmen.

Thomas played offensive line, defensive line, punter, tight end and even a little running back. Synold said he had the athleticism, as well as the proper grounding from his parents, to go far.

---

* Give Ciborowski credit here. He wasn't a bench jockey simply in awe of Thomas. A running back, Ciborowski would go on to play Division I football at Miami University in Ohio.

One of Thomas' coaches at Central, Scott Nelson, remembered Thomas' versatility on the field.* "It was all about getting him involved as much as possible," he said. Johnson even remembered between plays Thomas had to switch jerseys to make sure he wore the eligible number for the position he was being sent in to play. The jersey would hang like a poncho, he said.

As a tight end, "he was phenomenal because he had great hands, because he's a basketball player with really good hands," Nelson said. "Notre Dame, I think, offered him the keys to the kingdom as a sophomore as a tight end. And then, in spite of that, he was still willing to help the team (on the offensive line). He was right tackle because we were right dominant. In a running-style offense, that was a more crucial spot."

Eric Thomas credits his son's "big arm span and quick feet" for his success on the field, and "I always thought that what he learned in track in the shot and discus and what he learned as a soccer goalie made him a good lineman in football."

Much has been written advocating that young athletes play multiple sports rather than concentrating on only one. For one thing, different muscles are used, thereby allowing for better healing rather than overuse, which can lead to injuries.

"I could see how the footwork for track was helping him with his drop step in basketball. And I could see the foot speed of the game as a soccer goalie was helping him in basketball," Eric Thomas said. "In my head it kind of blended together that he benefits physically from having different training in different sports, as opposed to trying to focus on one and getting pigeonholed as a lineman or a running back or a tight end."

Nelson credited his colleague Jamie Meulemans as being the first to suggest moving Thomas from tight end to offensive tackle. The coaches brainstormed, and when they talked to Thomas they found a willing recipient.

---

* Oddly, in the rosters for the state football championship in 2002, Thomas was listed at two different weights — 6-7, 255 at right tackle and 265 on the defensive side. He also was down as the team's punter, averaging 38 yards per kick.

"But I think he made more of an impact as a defensive end, for the majority of his senior year, maybe even more than as an offensive lineman," Nelson said.

As a senior, Thomas earned co-defensive player-of-the-year honors with Portage's Justin Ostrowski. Thomas had 85 tackles and 12 sacks. (As a junior he had 70 tackles and eight sacks.) Think about that — he was named one of the state's two best defensive high school players yet starred on offense in college.

To become a better football player, Thomas worked hard not only on the field but off the field, too.

"Being a sponge, being a great student," Nelson said. "He already watched a lot of film in high school. So the fact that you'd hear these stories of him at Wisconsin watching film? Of course he is. And so that when he gets to the pros, and he's watching film, and knowing what defensive ends were going to do, none of us should be surprised. That's the way he was when he was 17."

Several games stand out for different reasons during Thomas' high school years.

"Our senior year, we played Verona in the state semifinals and won (9-6)," Strickland said "Offensively, we didn't have a great game. But that was the first time coaches yelled at him because he wasn't doing a great job on the back side climbing the linebackers, and basically washing those guys out of the picture so that I could cut back as a running back. And then the very next game was a state final game, and he just took over. And I think that was where I realized that when Joe turned it on, he was really, really different."

For Meulemans and Nelson, another game stood out, and it wasn't because of Thomas' play on the line.

"You don't see many offensive linemen or defensive ends who happen to be the punter, and he was a really good punter," Nelson said.

Central had faced rival East on the road in the second round of the playoffs.

In the fourth quarter, Central was backed up and punting with the score tied at 10. The team's long snapper, playing with a broken rib, snapped the ball high. "If Joe wasn't 6-8 and athletic . . ." Nelson recalls., "He went up as high as he could, grabs the ball — literally, probably at 10 and a half, 11 feet. Pulls it down, kicks it. It would have gone over his head. We were backed up. It would have probably gotten into the end zone, might have been a touchdown for them. He saved the game by being a punter."

Even opposing coaches were quick to laud Thomas. Before a state matchup in Thomas' senior year, Menomonie High School coach Joe LaBuda — one of the winningest coaches in Wisconsin state history — noted Brookfield Central had three Division I-caliber players, referring to Thomas and two of his pals, linebacker Johnson and running back Strickland. On Thomas, LaBuda told The Dunn County News, "He is widely regarded as the best offensive [or] defensive lineman in the Midwest. . . . He's very athletic. He's a great puller as an offensive lineman, which is very uncommon for a guy that size. . . . He's a very athletic 6-7. That's a great way to describe him. That's why everyone is so interested in him. When he pulls, he pulls like a 200-pound kid. And he's very quick for 6-7. He also is a standout defensive end. It's very difficult to run to his side of the ball."

Pulling requires speed from an offensive lineman. To the uninitiated, it looks like offensive linemen and defensive linemen simply smash into each other. But there is a choreography involved. If the offense runs the ball to the right, an offensive lineman on the left side often will run behind his teammates to pave the way for the running back.

For the record, Menomonie beat Central — but Thomas played up to LaBuda's praise.*

Thomas was receiving a lot of praise for his football play. But one person did more than just praise — he acted on it. Joe's pal Luke Homan decided he would be Joe's agent.

"'Oh, OK, you can be my agent,' "Joe told his friend, accord-

---

* Menomonie, never behind in the game, would win, 17-14. Thomas had two sacks, was in on six tackles, and punted.

ing to Sally Thomas' recollection. Homan wasn't exactly kidding. "So Luke pulls out this piece of paper that says 'I, Joe Thomas, I'm going to have Luke (as my agent) and I'm going to pay him some high percentage' and then Joe signs the thing," Sally recalls. "They must have been really young, but then for years Luke's carrying this around so then people are really looking at him — he'd be pulling this paper out. That used to bug Joe. 'Look, I'm gonna be his agent.' Joseph didn't like that later. His dad told him, 'You've got to watch what you're signing.'"

The media had also taken notice of Joe Thomas. The Milwaukee Journal Sentinel named him lineman of the year. He was first-team all state. The Detroit Free Press tabbed Thomas on their Best of the Midwest team. USA Today named him second-team All-American.

Joe would play in high school all-star games, including the 2003 U.S. Army All-American Bowl. The showcase drew top Division I prospects like Chris Leak, who would announce during the game he would attend Florida. It also featured a dozen players who eventually made it to the NFL. How good of a game did Thomas and his linemates have? Going up against the best of their peers on the other side of the ball, the East all-stars crushed the West, 47-3.

During the game, Thomas blocked for quarterback Brady Quinn, a Dublin, Ohio, product who was on his way to Notre Dame. It would be the first of several parallel connections between the two. But that would come a few years down the road. For some time, the recruiters had been calling, and Thomas would have a decision to make.

Coaches were seeing how good Thomas was first-hand. And no one had a better vantage than the coaches at Brookfield Central.*

Jeff Gryzwa remembers hosting a party at his house early in Thomas' high school playing days. Nelson attended.

"It was just a little teacher gathering," Gryzwa said. "And I

---

* Thomas is not the sole Brookfield Central alumnus to make it to the NFL. Steve Avery (class of '84) and Brad Nortman (class of '08) also played.

remember Scott saying that Joe is going to play on Sundays. I mean, he was that good in high school."

After Thomas graduated high school, Joe Panos, one of his former coaches, gave an interview to longtime Wisconsin sportswriter Mike Lucas. Panos was a former offensive tackle at Wisconsin who helped coach the offensive line at Brookfield Central. A walk-on, he served as a captain on Wisconsin's 1993 Rose Bowl team and played in the NFL for six seasons with Philadelphia and Buffalo.

"I had the players going through a bag drill, a reaction drill," he said. "I'm standing in front and pointing to the direction that I want them to go laterally over these bags. I say 'Go left, go right, go left, go right, go left, go stop and go.' And here's Joe just flying through the drill. I turned and looked at my assistants and said, 'This kid is going to play football for as long as he wants.'"

6

BEING RECRUITED:
A WANTED MAN

"Name a college, and they were here," recalls Scott Nelson, a math teacher and football coach at Brookfield Central High School. "I thought the Nebraska guy was going to get his own cot. He was here every day, all the time."

They were after Joe Thomas.

"Everybody wanted to have him," Nelson said. "So it was quite a situation. Most of them wanted him as an offensive lineman, but every once in a while someone would say, 'And if that doesn't work out, he's a pretty good defensive end, also.'"

Actually, he was being recruited in all three sports.

Colleges do as much homework as they can on a prospect, and that includes their grades and off-the-field behavior. They want to know that the guy they are recruiting is a student they don't have to worry about, if he coasted through with Bs and Cs, or if he were barely making it. For schools recruiting Thomas, academics wasn't an issue. He had a 3.5 grade-point average and scored 24 on his ACT and 1,200 on the SAT.

Ronn Blaha, a math teacher and basketball announcer at Brookfield Central, said Thomas asked him for a letter of recommendation to the University of Wisconsin. Thomas, who took precalculus with Blaha, was going through the process with UW like any normal student. "Because he didn't use one of the exemptions that Division I schools have for athletes who might not get admitted under the normal way, he asked me for a letter of recommendation, because he had to go through the regular admission process so they didn't have to use that exemption. I still have the piece of paper with the handwritten note, 'Can you write a letter of recommendation for me, Joe Thomas.'"

Blaha described Thomas as a "great student" who was engaged in class and did his homework. "It wasn't just being a jock. He wanted to know math and wanted to get high standards. He wanted to get an A."

With Thomas, colleges were looking at a solid student who had excelled at multiple sports. It was simply a question of what — and where — Thomas wanted to play.

"The funny thing about his recruiting was I think everybody thought along the way that he was going to go football but until we got into his junior year, Joe and his parents kept telling me to take all the calls on basketball because, 'We really haven't decided yet,'" said Mark Adams, his high school basketball coach.

During a summer tournament at the University of Milwaukee-Wisconsin, a college basketball coach approached Adams. "He just said, 'Let us know. We hear he wants to go football, but let us know because we'd love to have him here (for basketball).'"

Another Division I school also was interested in Thomas playing hoops. Adams couldn't recall the school but said an assistant in charge of recruiting "was calling me every other week, during the offseason, just to keep an eye on things." Adams kept the door open because Joe hadn't decided. But as soon as he chose football schools found out by word of mouth immediately, he said.

"When he told me — and I can't remember exactly when it was — he said, 'Hey, I think I'm gonna go with football.' And then I call the people who had been calling regularly and then anybody else who had called, and I told them. But it was funny how the word got out. You know, when I called a couple of schools, they said, 'Yeah, we heard already.'"

Adams believes Thomas could easily have played Division I basketball.

But football was the sport Thomas loved watching the most,

having grown up following the Packers on television. He doesn't remember the moment when he realized he was good enough to play Division I football or when he opted for a scholarship in that sport over the others.

"Honestly, I never really considered it because I just didn't let myself think that far down the line," Thomas said. "I think my parents did a good job of having me stay focused on school and what's in front of me and having fun, being a good teammate, that type of stuff. And so it really wasn't until I started getting offers, and I was, 'Wow, this is real. This is not fake anymore. I can actually maybe do this in college.'"

Central coaches were like parents trying to fend off suitors for a beautiful daughter. The courting was nonstop while they were trying to coach sports and teach classes.

At home, though, Eric Thomas, an analytical, measured person, took a different approach. "I set up a spreadsheet. And I told people when they called that we're in the collecting-information phase and send me the information on your team, your school, why you think Joe would be a good fit. And at a certain point, we're going to sit down with Joe and go through these and he'll pick his top five or seven. And we'll narrow it down and then we'll take personal visits. But please don't call him at home. Please don't go to the school. His education is important to us. And we will take you off the list if we find that you're not going along with these terms."

The final decision would be entirely Joe's, his parents said. But to get there, schools were going to have to play by the Thomas household rules.

To some degree, schools did not obey: Central coaches said a flood of coaches visited.

"It was a very, very stressful time," Sally Thomas said. "It was before cellphones, thankfully. But we had to get a dedicated line for a dial-up computer because there was lots of communication that way. And as I remember there were rules [regarding] when coaches could call and when they couldn't call. . . . He was mostly in the kitchen with a landline. No calls after 9 o'clock."

A Miami Hurricanes recruiter arrived at the school unannounced and told a coach they wanted to talk to Thomas. He was taking a physics test. He also had other important concerns: Prom was coming, as was fishing with his grandfather.

Nelson — once a University of Michigan fan — remembers that school did not come after Thomas as fervently as other schools. One time at a football clinic he ran into a Michigan coach, and Nelson told him, "'Hey, you recruited one of our guys. We're really proud of him. We love him. I think he's gonna be great.' And I remember him saying, 'Yeah, we think there's other guys . . . he might be OK, but you know, we're just not that high on him. We'll see how it works out.' And honestly, I went home and burned all my Michigan stuff. . . . I was just done with them."

Thomas also remembers Michigan not recruiting him much. Ohio State also didn't show much interest.

Eric and Sally Thomas knew Joe wanted to continue with both football and shot put. Not all recruiters seemed as concerned with what their son wanted. At least one coach who visited wanted Thomas on defense. While that wasn't a crazy thought — he had been co-high school player of the year in the state on defense — it wasn't what Thomas was leaning toward.

As Sally recalls, "Eric said, 'You have to explain you want to do both of these and ask the guy, what will this look like, you know, how will I do this if I come play for you?' And the guy was kind of hemming and hawing, and he called back and said, 'If you think you're missing spring ball, you got another thing coming.' So Joseph said, 'I don't think I want to go play for him.' So we're, 'Fine, you know, tell him no.' So he gets on the phone with this guy. And I think (Eric) told him, 'Just don't tell them why. Just tell them it's not a good fit. Don't not give them any reason to hang on to something to start badgering you.'"

Thomas did it. But it wasn't fun.

"He got off the phone and said, 'That was terrible,'" Sally said.

"That was the first time that Joe learned the art of saying no and the pushback," Eric recalls.

That moment of being told no is when a school faces a decision. They have an opportunity to wish a player good luck, or they can give the prospect the "You'll never get a good job in this town again and you'll be blacklisted" treatment.

That's not to say every situation resulted in a bad recruiting experience, and for a while Thomas was on the fence between sports. Thomas said he had a good relationship with the throws coach at Virginia Tech. Colorado and Kansas also went after him for track.

The Ken Carman and Anthony Lima podcast referred to a story with Thomas' high school coach Rick Synold, who was quoted saying Wisconsin and Cal wanted him as a tight end; USC as tight end or offensive lineman; Purdue and Iowa on defense; and Northwestern as an offensive lineman.

Holy Cross wanted him for basketball, and he received letters from Connecticut, Marquette and Wisconsin.

"But I think they saw the recruiting I was getting for football," Thomas said, "and then they just quickly realized, 'Hey, 6-7 white guy, can't really shoot from the outside, isn't really worth spending any of our time on. He's got big-time football offers. It looks like he's probably going to do that.'"

One newspaper at the time reported Thomas was being recruited by Wisconsin, Michigan, Iowa, USC and Stanford — five schools from two solid conferences — schools that regularly landed in bowl games.

"At first he was, 'Stanford, I'm going to Stanford,'" Sally Thomas said. "He wanted to go as far away as he possibly could. But we kept saying, 'Well, you can't come home at Thanksgiving. And you probably won't come home at Christmas.'"

Attending a school, 2,100 miles away would have been tough.

"My parents were probably Joseph's largest and most ardent fans," Sally said. "Joseph and my mother were very close when he was little. When he had to pick somebody to wear his jersey for a game, it was always for grandma. . . . I think he started thinking, 'Wow, if I go to Stanford or I go to Virginia Tech or I go wherever, none of my family's going to come.' And we were a very big part of his rooting section. And then all of a sudden he's looking at Notre Dame and Wisconsin.

"I always liked Notre Dame because I like the religious aspect," Sally said. "And Joseph kept saying, 'I can't go there, it's just too much like Marquette,' who was our rival high school. We would talk a lot at dinner, you know, 'Where are you going to go?' And (one night) we're gone and Billy (Thomas' younger brother) answers the phone. And some reporter is asking him all these questions — you know, 'What's your inside scoop? Where is he going to go?' And he must have said something like, 'Well, my mom likes Notre Dame' or something about Notre Dame. So the guy writes that Joseph is going to go to Notre Dame. We didn't know this happened. Why would they think he's going to Notre Dame? Where do you get that idea?"

Billy said, "'I think it might have been my fault. I think I might have said something,'" Sally remembered.

Interestingly, the only time a shred of doubt about Joe's future might have crept into Eric Thomas' psyche came on the Notre Dame visit.

The Irish wanted Thomas as a tight end. His weight fluctuated, about 265 for football but leaner for basketball. The visit to South Bend came during basketball season and Eric said he looked "skinny."

"We had a great visit to Notre Dame," Eric said. Sally's sister-in-law's nephew played for them, and Joe was introduced to him. "He was about 6-9, 340 pounds. And then standing next to him is Joe in basketball shape. And I'm thinking 'He better grab the first thing that comes along because there's just no way he can compete with people who are that big.' It was kind of one of those, 'Whoo, if he can get into Notre Dame, great education.'"

The school's facilities might also have been a factor.

"Notre Dame at the time had a weight room from the '40s — dark, dingy, old equipment," Eric said. "And you know, you go to Nebraska and everything is state of the art. You go to Wisconsin, everything is state of the art. And Notre Dame just didn't match up facilitywise at the time."

The coach, though, was a positive. "Coach (Ty) Willingham — a silent, 'Do as I do, don't just do as I say.' He was great man of faith. I would have been proud to have Joe play for him."

Things got "sort of ugly with Notre Dame people," Adams recalls. "Because it pretty much came down to Notre Dame and Wisconsin, and I think Notre Dame thought being an elite program nationally that they were going to, you know, reel him in. And when it didn't happen, they were pretty upset."

Paul Chryst, a tight ends coach at the time, was the main person recruiting Thomas from Wisconsin.* He visited the Thomas home.

"Such a great man," Sally Thomas recalls. She said Chryst sat down with Wisconsin's head football coach, Barry Alvarez, and went over the schedule for the two sports. Then, he presented it to Joe and his parents. "He was going to be allowed to miss spring ball in order to play. I truly believe that's when Joseph thought, 'This is where I want to go.'"

Some recruits are sold on the glamour of the game, and especially schedules that offer visibility on national television, to have a realistic chance to compete for a national championship, to play for a high-profile school with big name coaches for potential NFL draft exposure. Thomas was motivated by the school being willing to let him also compete in track and field.

Alvarez was being open-minded.

"Barry used to always say 'Can't let any of those guys get out of this state.' That's their bread and butter," Sally Thomas said. (In Joe's freshman season, 2003-04, about 40 percent of the Badgers' football roster hailed from Wisconsin.)

Adams remembers Alvarez's visit to Brookfield Central.

---

* A story by Robert Mays, formerly of Grantland, revealed a sliver of the recruiting process from Chryst's perspective: "It's typical for coaches to see a recruit compete in a different sport as a sign of moral support and a show of commitment," Mays wrote. He tells how Chryst went to see Thomas, then a high school junior, compete in track. Thomas launched the shot almost 64 feet. Chryst didn't know much about shot put, but he noticed that Thomas' reaction was lukewarm. The next day, Chryst went to another school to see another recruit throw. After the young man's toss barely cleared 50 feet, Chryst walked over and patted him on the shoulder, told him to hang in there. The kid looked at Chryst and said, "Coach, I just set a school record and a personal best."

"I get a little leery sometimes that somebody's going to go so gung-ho with their sport, in this case football, that they might discourage somebody from doing the other sports," he said. "And the last thing that Alvarez said, he looked at the three of them (Thomas, Ben Strickland and Steve Johnson). He says, 'And I expect to see you on that basketball court in Madison watching you (guys) at the state tournament.' I thought that was really cool."

Mike Lucas, a sportswriter with The Capital Times in Madison, said Wisconsin was aware that Thomas was being heavily recruited and was a versatile football prospect. "I think even Wisconsin considered during the recruiting process that, 'Look, this guy can play tight end.'"

Jamie Meulemans, a teacher and offensive coordinator when Thomas was at Central, said Thomas already had Olympic aspirations in shot put. And as soon as Alvarez and company got wind that Kansas wanted him for track, Wisconsin made sure the message was clear: He could play both sports.

The recruiting circus was "pretty crazy," Thomas told the South Bend Tribune, "but I look at it as a privilege. It's people wanting you, and you're in control. They're courting you. It's a great thing."

When the dust settled, Wisconsin was the clear favorite, with Notre Dame a distant second.*

Jeff Gryzwa, a teacher at Central and friend of Thomas — the two hunted together—said he wrote letters of recommendation for Wisconsin, Notre Dame and Stanford. But he couldn't help putting up a poster of Wisconsin, since he was a season ticket holder, and he made sure Thomas saw it as a not-so-subtle nudge. Gryzwa said Thomas called him at two or three in the morning when he decided on Wisconsin.

---

* How did things work out for Notre Dame and Wisconsin? In 2002, Notre Dame finished 10-3. In 2003, after Thomas opted for Wisconsin, the Irish went 5-7. In 2004, as Thomas was winding down his sophomore year bolstering the offensive line for the Badgers, Notre Dame was on its way to a 6-6 record. Ty Willingham was fired. Hindsight is 20-20, but things were going swimmingly for Wisconsin. In the time Thomas was in college, Notre Dame went to three bowl games, losing all of them.

Not long after Thomas chose Wisconsin, Gryzwa ran into Alvarez at an event. "You're getting a good guy," he told the Wisconsin coach. "And what Barry told me was if they got him, it was going to be a good class coming in. I mean, he was their main focal point. And I told Barry, 'Just so you know, he's a punter, too.' I told Joe that, and Joe said, 'Don't tell him that.'"

The trips to visit schools helped Thomas put his decision in perspective.

"When I was away, I really realized what my family means to me and what the state of Wisconsin means to me and how much I really love being here," he told the Wisconsin State Journal. "I really like the idea of playing for your home state and playing in front of your home fans."

On Feb. 5, 2003, Joe Thomas — wearing a University of Wisconsin football shirt — signed his letter of intent.

"Back then people didn't really make as much of a big deal about your announcement. I told the schools — you know, the guys that didn't get it," Thomas said. "And then I told Wisconsin. I think I called Paul (Chryst). On signing day, I came to the cafeteria or the gym, and the pep band was there, and you did the official signing. I remember there was never a big announcement.

Thomas' choice to attend Wisconsin would be a perfect fit — for him and the school. Neither would have regrets.

PART TWO

ON, WISCONSIN!

7

HEADING TO MADISON
2003-04

*On, Wisconsin! On, Wisconsin! Plunge right
through that line!
Run the ball clear down the field, a touchdown sure this time.*
— "On, Wisconsin!" fight song

In 2003, Joe Thomas arrived at the scenic campus nestled along Lake Mendota in Madison, a city of 250,000. For a fisherman, the water beckoned. But where he would make his mark would be inside the venerable Camp Randall.

One of the nation's oldest football stadiums, Camp Randall remains an electrifying and historic place to watch a college football game. The land where the stadium sits originally was owned by the Wisconsin Agricultural Society and served as the site of the annual state fair. It became a military training center for Civil War troops and is named for Alexander W. Randall, Wisconsin's governor at that time. After the war, it reverted to state fair property. The fair eventually moved to Milwaukee, and in 1893 it was declared a memorial athletic field.

Football started at UW in 1889. The fight song "On, Wisconsin!" originally was written to be the fight song for the University of Minnesota — ironic considering the neighboring state schools have been playing each other annually since 1890 with only one missed game, in 1906.

Collapse of the bleachers in 1915 led to a more permanent stadium with concrete stands. In 1917, it opened as a 10,000-seat stadium. Over the years, the stadium underwent renovations and additions, including a 1964 project directed by Osborn Engineering of Cleveland. It now seats more than 80,000.

In William Campbell Gault's 1953 young-adult sports-fiction book, "Mr. Fullback," the stadium is the site of a Wisconsin victory over the fictitious Marlowe squad. The Milwaukee native author attended nearby Wauwatosa High School.

It also is home to one of college football's traditions, the Fifth Quarter, as thousands stay to hear the marching band play a variety of traditional and modern songs.

The highly recruited Thomas came in with a long list of preseason pats on the back. Every college football analyst had him somewhere on their lists of rated prospects. Tom Lemming ranked him as the nation's No. 4 offensive tackle coming out of high school. Rivals.com had him high on their lists, including pegging him as the No. 3 player in Wisconsin. Most players at Division I schools have some sort of a resume, but Thomas was lauded mostly for his play on the defensive side in high school yet here he was about to line up on offense. The player he shared the Wisconsin Football Coaches Association 2002 Defensive Player of the Year honors with — Justin Ostrowski — also landed in Madison that fall.

"We kind of knew he was coming," quarterback John Stocco said. "He had been racking up accolades in both track and football. And so I think most guys were aware that this guy can be pretty good."

Thomas had grown up a fan of the Badgers, though without cable TV in the family home he hadn't watched them much on television. Thomas, though, didn't wear his resume on his sleeve when he took to the practice field as a college freshman. He was honest about his learning curve.

"The first day (in pads) I had a lot of trouble," he told Mike Lucas, who covered Wisconsin for The Capital Times and who would go on to become radio color commentator for Wisconsin games.

"Obviously the speed is so much faster. You're used to a guy being here. Instead, he's 2 yards past that. Obviously, I want to get bigger and stronger — I'm between 275 and 280. I have enough confidence that I think I can play with anybody who's coming up against me and that's the most important thing."

He learned fast.

On only the sixth day of practice Thomas took repetitions with the second team and a few with the first.

"He will be as good as he wants to be in his career," head coach Barry Alvarez told Wisconsin State Journal writer Tom Mulhern. "I don't think anyone's disappointed in what they've seen. He's a mature individual, he's very smart, he picks things up, he absorbs it and he's athletic enough to make corrections."

Any possibility of redshirting Thomas was fading fast.*

On the afternoon of Aug. 30, 2003, Thomas took to the field for his first college game, 675 miles away in Morgantown, West Virginia. More than 60,000 fans turned out for the nonconference game, which was close. Wisconsin used a late drive to pull out a 24-17 win after being down 10.

Thomas had played as a backup left tackle in training camp but got in the game and made the most of his time, about 10 plays. He served as an extra blocker in the second half to help pave the way for running back Anthony Davis, who rushed for 167 yards.

"The first couple of plays, I thought it was pretty neat to actually be playing in a game in college in front of so many people," Mulhern quoted Thomas as saying. "After that, I settled down a little bit and did my job pretty well, hopefully. The biggest thing was I couldn't even hear the quarterback's snap count. I'm not used to that. Even in practice you are simulating crowd noise and you could hear him just a little bit, but I couldn't hear him at all. So, I had to just watch the ball and play the ball. That was the hardest

---

* Redshirting is the act of sitting a player for a season, often when they are injured or early in their career when they are still learning. The rule of thumb is a player has a window of usually five years to play four, though COVID eligibility, transfer rules and other exceptions can be made.

thing for me right off the bat because (otherwise) I was pretty comfortable with what I was doing."*

Thomas often suited up as a blocking tight end in the Badgers' jumbo package. That formation often brings an extra tight end as a blocker in lieu of a receiver. His versatility eventually would serve him well as the Badgers settled into the season.

Thomas was a college coach's dream, since he played, and excelled at, multiple positions in high school. That would be a good thing because when the 7-5 Badgers accepted a bid to the Music City Bowl in Nashville against Auburn on Dec. 31, Thomas' adaptability would serve the team well.

Who starts and who plays in college is determined by coaches evaluating who is having solid practices, of course. But a domino effect results from injuries to other players. On Nov. 22, 2003, defensive end Darius Jones went down with a knee injury in Wisconsin's final regular-season game, a 27-21 loss to Iowa. That triggered the chain reaction that moved Thomas to defense.

Mulhern even reported that Thomas' pals on the offensive line jokingly called him "a traitor since he moved to the defensive line earlier in bowl practice." Center Donovan Raiola said, "We went out last night. We said, 'Oh, you want to hang out with us again?'"

Good-natured razzing aside, it showed a lot about Thomas, a freshman. Mulhern noted the importance of the timing of Thomas being shifted to defense: "It's amazing to think that Thomas, who had not played on the defensive line since high school . . . could

---

* After his retirement, Thomas said he experienced butterflies on occasion, as many athletes do. "I found that I perform at my best when I'm focused and calm. As offensive lineman, it's kind of important to have that clear mind. So I would actually close my eyes in the locker room, and that helped me visualize what I needed to do. In the middle of my career, when things started getting easier to me, it was almost counterproductive, because then I noticed that I didn't have enough energy. When the game would start and having just a little bit of nervousness helped with some of the focus inside, I would kind of start creating things in my head during the week about, 'Oh, this guy's really good, he's going to find a way to beat me.' You build your opponent up a little bit more than he actually is, to artificially build some of that nervousness and then steer that into a focus and an energy once the game started."

move to a new position and in the span of bowl practices move into the starting job."

Thomas wasn't fazed by the transition of being a freshman moving from offense to defense just prior to a bowl game. He told the Wisconsin State Journal: "It's a lot easier than offense. Learning the reads and the calls on the offensive line are so much more difficult than what you're doing on defense, where you're playing a reactionary position. Instincts help a lot. But there still are a lot of bad habits that I had in high school that I'm trying to correct."

Two weeks prior to the bowl on New Year's Eve 2003, Thomas was listed on the depth chart twice — as backup left offensive tackle to Morgan Davis and backup defensive end to Joe Monty.*

Auburn proved too much in the bowl game. Alvarez was denied his 100th victory at Wisconsin. On offense, the Tigers' running game pushed through Wisconsin. On defense, Auburn pressured quarterback Jim Sorgi on the way to a 28-14 victory. Thomas was in on eight tackles.

But Thomas's ability to shift to the other side of the line was not lost on Alvarez. "You'd like to have five Joe Thomases," he told the Wisconsin State Journal.

With the team sputtering along a mediocre season during Thomas' freshman year, Alvarez's words rang of both truth and a little frustration. With the bowl loss, Wisconsin would finish 7-6 in 2003. But better things were on the horizon.

---

* One day at practice, an incident took place with Joe Monty that surprised defensive coordinator Bret Bielema. "He and Joe are really good buddies, right? I mean, really good. And we're in fall camp, and we're kind of hitting the doldrums of fall camp, everybody getting anxious to play the other guy. In the middle of practice, there's this knock-down drag-out. Joe Monty and Joe Thomas are on the ground — two of my best players. They're in the middle of this pile, and they're just swinging, pushing people down, people trying to separate them. And I'm like, 'Jesus, guys, what in the world?' So I separated them. And I keep the two of them afterwards, because I know they're friends. 'Fellas, what are you two doing?' Joe looks at me and he looks at Joe Monty and he says: 'Coach, sometimes you just need a good fight to get things fired up around here.' I said, 'Absolutely, I get it.' We went on to have a pretty good season. I always go back to that moment. They had staged the whole thing. And they knew that everybody would react in a certain way because of who they are."

In March 2004, when Tom Mulhern of the Wisconsin State Journal asked about the potential of starting in his upcoming sophomore season, Thomas was succinct.

"I think I'm ready."

8

COMING INTO HIS OWN
2004-05

His sophomore year, Thomas roomed with his Brookfield Central teammates, Ben Strickland and Steve Johnson.

Before Thomas' sophomore season started, the Wisconsin State Journal printed a rather prescient nod. In the season preview the newspaper asked: "Is Thomas ready to take over at left tackle? All indications are Thomas is simply too talented to remain on the bench."

"It's very rare when you find special kids like him, he's just so gifted," defensive line coach John Palermo was quoted as saying. "Selfishly, I would love to have him, but I know he can be special at left tackle. He's not only athletic, but he's really a bright kid. You only have to tell him something once."

The door remained open, though, for Thomas to swing back to the defensive side, as he had done in the bowl game at the end of his freshman year. No one knew it then, but down the line, Thomas playing defense in bowl games would not always have the best outcome. Palermo was hoping Thomas might be able to help out in short-yardage and goal-line opportunities.

Meanwhile, Thomas was impressing on offense. He was the first true freshman offensive lineman to see action during Barry Alvarez's reign as head coach, which began in 1990. Right before the season, at media day in Chicago, Alvarez wasn't holding back.

Often, players at media-day events come across in a braggadocio manner while coaches temper things a bit — sometimes too much. Lou Holtz excelled at poor-mouthing — that is, saying how worried he was about an upcoming team, how tough the opponent is, how much work his guys had to do — and then going out on Saturday and winning by three touchdowns. But at media day it was Alvarez who sang the praises of his star lineman.

"I really think as a true sophomore (Thomas) has a chance to be as good an offensive lineman as we've had. He's probably the most athletic lineman we've had."

Thomas, in this continued day and age of swagger, took the humbler approach. "I think the key word there is 'could.' I haven't started a game on offense yet and haven't really played a snap at left tackle in a crucial moment. So there's definitely a lot of playing to do before anyone starts talking."

But coaches, teammates and the media were noticing a work ethic. Thomas was staying after practice to study film. He would focus on angles to get to linebackers as efficiently as possible. He also was doing well in the weight room, setting records for his position. In the hang clean — where a weight bar is pulled up to the chest in one motion — he lifted 405 pounds. Thomas also set strength-position records in the 40-yard dash (4.87 seconds), squat (620 pounds) and vertical jump (33.5 inches). The only record he didn't hold was in the bench press, held by former offensive lineman Chris McIntosh, who lifted 480 to Thomas' 410.*

He had earned that starting spot, and he beat out a guy who was no slouch at left tackle. Morgan Davis was a solid athlete, a hockey player-turned-football lineman who would be good enough to get a look with the Pittsburgh Steelers after college.

"Right now," Thomas said then, "my main goal is to leave camp with the starting left tackle spot." A key task: Protecting quarterback John Stocco.

---

* A former standout lineman, McIntosh went on to the NFL and in 2021 was named athletic director at Wisconsin. Longtime sportswriter Mike Lucas — who has been covering Badgers sports since the 1960s when he was on the school newspaper — tabbed both Thomas and McIntosh as two of the best offensive linemen to play at Wisconsin.

In its coverage, The Capital Times observed that Stocco "can rest easy, knowing that the UW's next superstar lineman, Joe Thomas, will protect your blind side with a passion."

The season kicked off with a convincing win against an atrocious Central Florida team, 34-6. It wasn't much of a test; the Golden Knights would go winless that year. After the game, offensive coordinator Brian White praised Thomas, saying "It's hard (for defenses) to prepare for his athletic ability. He's smart, he's tough, and he truly is a very, very unique athlete."

But White took the praise further, with a remarkable comment. "You probably heard this for the first time. We've got to game plan around a tackle like him, and we will." It wasn't hyperbole. White was talking about designing plays around an offensive lineman.

It's easy to understand why a team would create plays around a receiver who is the fastest guy on the field, conference or league. But an offensive lineman?

It was true. Stocco explained it.

"We put in that play where he would release and go block the corner. We also had a pass protection where we would have two tight ends in the game — you know, heavy personnel. We have two tight ends and running backs; we've got an eight-man protection. And we put in a max pass protection where it was designed to get three double-teams. So we're gonna double-team three of the four defensive linemen that we're going up against. But Joe was always singled up. Joe never got any help. And none of us were ever concerned about that. You know, me as a quarterback, I'm like, 'I don't care if Joe's singled up, I'm not gonna have any pressure.' So that was another thing that we put in specifically with Joe. Joe was singled up, and everybody else got double-team help."

Translated: The play's design allows the quarterback as much time as possible to throw when everyone in the stadium, from the opposing team to the hot-dog vendors, knows at that moment Wisconsin has to pass.

It was, as Stocco said, "a testament to Joe."

Offensive line is not a position that garners glory or multiple lines on a statistical sheet. Look at a box score for an offensive lineman and it's bare bones. But check out statistics for a Major League Baseball player, and the statistical categories read like alphabet soup mixed with the periodic table — acronyms upon acronyms with more seemingly being added all the time. Basketball has multiple categories for players to be evaluated, from offensive and defensive rebounds, to points, assists, steals, personal fouls and other categories — all affecting every player on the court. Football statistics are geared to the position: How many yards did a player throw for, how many rushing attempts, how many receptions? If he's on defense, how many sacks, tackles or tackles for loss? But look up an offensive lineman's stats and they are as minimalistic as you can get: Position, games started vs. played by season, jersey number worn and fumbles. He isn't gaining yards, he isn't catching passes (illegal in most cases), and he isn't making tackles.

Offensive linemen are kind of like baseball umpires who take grief when fans assume they blew a play — despite the fact the officials are correct in their calls well over 90 percent of the time.

"It really falls in line with the old cliché that if you don't really hear him, or he doesn't surface in front of your eyes, he's doing his job," former Capital Times sportswriter Mike Lucas said.

As Chris Lamb, an author of several sports books, says, "An offensive lineman does a job that no one notices until he does something wrong."

This was the role Thomas was relishing in.

Even as a college sophomore he exhibited a self-awareness. "The offensive line is not a glory position. If your running back is getting a lot of yards, people are going to say how great the back is and that the offensive line is doing a good job. But if you start allowing sacks and missing blocks, they're going to start singling you out."

Thomas' mother once told a reporter her son gravitated to the position: "He told me once that he wanted to be a left tackle. 'You aren't the quarterback, everybody's not out to get you. You just do your job and then you have the self-satisfaction that you did it right.'"

Thomas' consistent play ignored the score and the clock. While some guys might take a play or two off if they were up or down by a few touchdowns late in a game, there was no quit in Thomas. On Nov. 20, 2004, a 9-1 Wisconsin team traveled to face an 8-2 Iowa squad fighting for a share of the conference title. The Badgers were down 27-7 with a little more than 9 minutes remaining in the fourth quarter. Iowa's Chad Greenway pressured Stocco, knocking the ball loose. The Hawkeyes' Jonathan Babineaux scooped up the ball near his own 40 and headed for the end zone. It was Thomas — a lineman — who raced downfield and, as Wisconsin's last hope, caught Babineaux on the Wisconsin 25. "And Joe Thomas saved a touchdown," viewers hear.

As a sophomore, efforts like that propelled Thomas to honorable-mention nods on the All-Big Ten teams as voted by both coaches and media.

At the end of the season, Wisconsin met Georgia in the Outback Bowl. For the second consecutive year, the Badgers fell short in their bowl game. Stocco was pressured all game, and Wisconsin lost to the favored Bulldogs, 24-21. Despite finishing on a down note — the Badgers lost their final three games — Wisconsin wound up 9-3, a marked improvement over the previous season.

Mulhern of the Wisconsin State Journal estimated Thomas had been on the field for about 800 plays his sophomore year while giving up 1.5 to two sacks.

Thomas also was working hard at track and field. In competition, Thomas performed as if he had not been playing football but training solely for shot.

A month after the bowl game, Thomas competed in the Panther Classic in Cedar Falls, Iowa. He won the shot put with a heave of 59 feet, 5½ inches. At the Big Ten Conference indoor championships at Purdue, Thomas finished second while setting a school record of 62¼. The previous mark had stood since 1979.

"It just took off and I knew as soon as it left my fingers, I knew it was going to be a bomb," Thomas told the Wisconsin State Journal.

One of the selling points on Thomas attending Wisconsin was

the coaches' willingness to be amenable about him playing two sports. And in March 2005, he was excused from spring football practice to compete in an NCAA indoor track meet in Fayetteville, Arkansas. He threw 56 feet, 11 ½ inches and finished 14th.

Weeks later, competing in the Gatorade Classic in Knoxville, Tennessee, Thomas won the discus with a throw of 167-9 and finished second in shot put at 58-10¼.

Mark Napier, a Wisconsin track coach, lavished praise on Thomas. "He's extremely focused," he told Mulhern of the Wisconsin State Journal. "He's always on time on things. He's very structured. He doesn't miss his meetings in football. He doesn't miss his stuff in track. He's a parent's dream come true, because he's got such a humble personality and such a great commitment to everything he does."

That commitment apparently extended to using his time wisely for another passion — fishing.

"We went to a track meet at Long Beach State," said Thomas' mom, Sally. "The plane with the athletes flies out at the same time. And they have all the preliminaries in the beginning, but the shot and the disc athletes have two days of downtime, and then they start their preliminaries. And so Joe went on a group charter out on the bay and caught a bunch of fish. And this other kid bought a deep fryer and peanut oil. And then Joe paid to have the fish cleaned on the boat. And he bought tortillas and tartar sauce and they went back to the track meet. He plugged the deep fryer into the stadium lights, and boiled a fish fry and then rolled them up into tortillas and fed the team."

Thomas remembers the story: "There was a bunch of us, 10 or 12, who went out on one of these big head boats out of Malibu. It's basically just a big boat where they give you a big rod and they give you a bunch of bait and they pull up over a reef and maybe 250 feet of water. Everyone drops their bait to the bottom and whatever you catch you bring up. We had some excellent fishing. The captain actually said, 'This is one of the best days we've ever had.' So we just caught an unlimited amount of fish. We just took what we can eat for the day. We fried them up right there at the track meet on the sideline. Fed the whole track team."

In the Mideast Regional in Indianapolis in May 2005, Thomas finished third in the shot put with a toss of 62 feet, 3 inches, and qualified for NCAA Outdoor championships.

None of what Thomas was doing in football or track surprised his coaches — Bielema was aware of how good he was at track — or his competitors.

Brandon Houle, who first competed against Thomas in high school while attending Oshkosh North, and then later with him on the track team at Wisconsin, understood the demands it took to be a world-class athlete.

"I never count him out. He will always find a way to attain what he's looking to do. And I would agree that doing two sports in college is an insane amount of time. While you have guys who are not in football and just focusing on track, like myself, I can spend all that extra time focusing on my craft and trying to get better. He doesn't have that luxury. Had he focused just purely on track, I don't think there's any doubt in my mind that he would have been an Olympian and eventually gotten a medal. I think that he had the talent and he had the drive and he had the skills to definitely do it, for sure."

Coaches marveled. Media took notice. And Thomas was having fun.

"I'm a competitor. I just love competing. I love sports," he said. "Right now, I'm having a blast."

9

A NATIONAL SPOTLIGHT SHINES

2005-06

Thomas started his junior year with an additional role: runway model. OK, it was a one-time thing, but the 6-8 lineman was one of several players chosen to show off the Badgers' new alternate uniforms (which harkened to the early to mid-1960s with simple dark cardinal-colored jerseys and a giant "W" on the front of the helmets) at a preseason media event in August.

The season looked promising for Wisconsin. Despite the tail-off at the end of the 2004 season, Alvarez had the Badgers in good shape and poised for their fourth consecutive bowl bid.

For his part, Thomas was ready. He didn't even mind running "stadiums," the steep, leg-churning uphill conditioning runs, which he did while listening to AC/DC or Metallica.

As the season started, Thomas was in fine form, and he immediately began living up to the hyperbole-pushing preseason praise the coaches had heaped on him.

Wisconsin won a shootout, 56-42, over Bowling Green in the season opener at Camp Randall. Running back Brian Calhoun riddled the Falcons' defense, rushing 43 times for 258 yards and a school-record five touchdowns. On a fourth-and-1 play, he raced 20 yards for a touchdown thanks to Thomas' blocking. The Wisconsin coaches, though, named Calhoun *and* Thomas co-offensive players of the week.

Calhoun came to Wisconsin as a transfer from Colorado, but he was homegrown, having played high school ball at Oak Creek in the Milwaukee suburbs. After two years with Colorado, he joined the Badgers at a perfect time. From 2001 to 2004, Anthony Davis had gained 4,676 yards with Wisconsin and was a final-round draft choice of the Indianapolis Colts. Calhoun was a versatile running back who also ran track. Thomas said the team was lucky to have him.

Calhoun was lucky, too — to have someone of Thomas' caliber blocking for him.

But it soon turned out Thomas might be doing more than blocking. When early-season injuries on the defensive line mounted for the Badgers, Bielema told Thomas he might be needed on defense for goal-line stands, and maybe at defensive end. (Thomas had started at defensive end in the 2003 Music City Bowl against Auburn.)

"Maybe in special occasions. Last week, we had him ready if need be for a goal-line situation," Alvarez told The Capital Times after the team started 3-0 in 2005. "It might be for a play here or there, if in an emergency. That would be the only way."

The coaches weren't poor-mouthing. The Badgers' defensive line had lost four players to the NFL draft that spring. Jamal Cooper tore an ACL in the Badgers' third game of the season. Justin Ostrowski was out with a knee injury. And backup Mark Gorman had broken his leg before the season.

Thomas couldn't control what was happening on defense, but he could continue to work on his offensive game. He considered himself a perfectionist. Like many college students, Thomas spent Sunday afternoons watching NFL games. But instead of focusing on the running backs, quarterbacks or receivers, he watched the offensive linemen, picking up footwork and other techniques to use in his own upcoming games.

When Wisconsin's Big Ten opener against Michigan rolled around on Sept. 24, one of the key matchups the media focused on was Joe Thomas against defensive end LaMarr Woodley — a classic conflict of immovable object vs. unstoppable force. Going into the game, Woodley had 12 tackles on the season, including three for loss and two sacks.

In the end, it was a good one. Woodley was in on eight tackles and credited with half a sack. But the Badgers won, 23-20. Calhoun rushed for 155 yards, thanks in large part to Thomas.

"The best player I played against in my college career was LaMarr Woodley," Thomas said years later, after his NFL career, while talking about the jump in talent from college to the NFL. Woodley went on to have a solid NFL career, Thomas noted. "But playing against him in college, I made a name for myself because he was such a great college player. If you have a good game against him, pro scouts are going to be knocking on the door, thinking that you can play in the NFL."

Playing well against defensive stars is one way to catch the eye of scouts. But how well your running backs are doing also says a lot about an offensive lineman. And going into an early October game at home vs. Indiana, Brian Calhoun was averaging 157 yards per game — third best in Division I.

A week later, Wisconsin took a 5-0 record and a No. 14 ranking to Evanston, Illinois, to face Northwestern. The Badgers scored 48 points — and lost. Wisconsin's defense allowed 51 points against an unranked opponent.

But there was one particularly notable moment. Wisconsin called a Whammer screen, a play designed to look like a run. It called for Thomas to take a couple of steps outside, find the cornerback and, well, obliterate him. That's what happened: 5-10, 185-pound cornerback Deante Battle was pulverized on the play. Afterward, Thomas told a reporter: "He didn't talk much. I don't think that he wanted to see me anymore." That play might have taken some sting out of the loss.

National awards are resume notches that can put a player on an NFL team's radar, just like an academic award can catch someone's eye in an interview. Thomas already had received attention from writers who were covering Wisconsin, but being nominated for the Lombardi Award brought him into more of a national spotlight. Of the semifinalists for the award, which honors a lineman, eight were on the defensive side; only four were offensive linemen.

Purdue coach Joe Tiller described Thomas to the Associated Press, "He looks to me like he's out of the cookie-cutter production line at Wisconsin."

Teammate Dontez Sanders (who is from Bedford, Ohio, and attended St. Peter Chanel High School), marveled in an Associated Press story: "He has no fat on him. He looks like a linebacker or tight end."

In a 35-14 loss to Penn State, the Badgers lost the battle in the trenches, though Thomas was noted for his play. Tamba Hali, the Nittany Lions' outstanding defensive end who would go on to an All-Pro NFL career, had his way in various matchups, except for one. In the few times he matched up with Hali, Thomas held his own. Thomas, one reporter wrote, was the only player the Wisconsin coaches "felt comfortable leaving" in one-on-one matchups vs. Hali.* For his part, Thomas wanted more. "I think when he lined up there," he said, "I gave him everything I've got."

With all-Big Ten Conference selections out and a game at Hawaii approaching, projections had Thomas going in the first 20 positions in the NFL draft. An estimate of where in the draft a player might be taken figures into that player's decision whether to stay in school or turn pro. "It gets harder (to return) the further up they say," Thomas told Mulhern.

"It wasn't until my junior year when scouts started to come to practices. And they started asking me about whether I was considering going out early. And I was: 'What? Go out early?' I didn't even think I could play in the NFL much less (be a top draft choice). Why would I leave after my junior year? And then by the end of my junior year they had asked me if I was leaving and that I should go and do the junior application where they kind of tell you what your

---

* Not long after the Penn State game, a mock draft report forecast Thomas going 20th in the first round to Tampa Bay in the 2006 NFL draft. At the time, Thomas had not made up his mind on declaring for the draft. When the draft rolled around, it would be Tamba Hali who went to Kansas City with the No. 20 pick.

draft status is. So I did that to see what happens. And it came back (showing) I'd be the second tackle selected behind D'Brickashaw Ferguson, probably first round or somewhere.* I was, 'Wow.' That kind of blew me away. And then I think from that point on I started getting a little bit more serious — like, this is probably going to be my profession."

Draft hype wasn't Thomas' only claim to fame.

Late in the 2005 season, The Capital Times ran a feature on Gabe Carimi, a standout high school recruit from the Milwaukee area. Carimi would commit to Wisconsin, where he would have a great career and go on to the NFL. In the story, the then-high schooler listed his role models: his parents — and Joe Thomas.

In a story with the Wisconsin State Journal, Carimi said: "He is, quote-unquote, my hero. I really want to model myself after his size and how big he is. I'd really like to be like Joe Thomas."

When all-conference selections were announced, Thomas was on the first team on both the coaches' and the media's lists.

"This definitely feels good. It's a step, but it's not the end, that's for sure," Thomas told Mulhern.

It also wasn't the end of the season for Wisconsin. The Badgers were headed for the Capital One Bowl to face the Auburn Tigers, who had beaten them two years earlier in the Music City Bowl.

The casualty tally was growing on the defensive side. In the Badgers' regular season finale (a win over Hawaii the day after Thanksgiving, lifting the Badgers' record to 9-3), defensive end

---

* After Thomas had petitioned the NFL for a draft evaluation, a top-15 pick was forecast for him. The 2006 draft's top offensive lineman did turn out to be D'Brickashaw Ferguson of Virginia. Ferguson and Thomas would have something in common more than just a shared position and first-round selection: A snap streak. In the 2006 draft — the one Thomas was considering entering — the New York Jets selected Ferguson as the No. 4 overall pick. Like Thomas, he would go on to a stellar professional career. Ferguson played 10,707 of 10,708 regular-season snaps. In a 2008 game he was removed so the Jets could run a multiple lateral trick play — the rugby-like desperation gambit probably more enjoyable for fans than players. The play failed — and put the brakes on Ferguson's streak. The coach who pulled Ferguson was Eric Mangini, who was the Browns' head coach for the 2009-10 seasons.

Travis Beckum became the latest to go down, leaving the game after getting hit in the knee with a helmet. "I don't know where we're going to go with all the defensive linemen we keep losing," Alvarez told the Capital Times . . . We might have to dust off Joe Thomas (to play defense) for the bowl game."

Defensive line coach John Palermo was more direct. After the Hawaii game he told Thomas: Prepare to play defense. The plan would be 10 to 15 plays on probable runs. Thomas took the increased playing time in stride. Coupled with 65 to 70 plays on offense, it would be "a large game," he told Mulhern. "I think that would be reasonable to expect that out of myself."

Alvarez said at the time he could not recall any offensive linemen who could play defensive end. A heck of a comment from someone whose career started in the early 1970s as a high school coach, and who had stints at Iowa and Notre Dame (and who would wind up at Wisconsin for 16 full seasons as head coach).

The jobs of the two linemen are inherently different. Offensive linemen are the biggest players on the field. Defensive linemen give up some weight and gain speed. The two meet, play after play, in successive car crashes at the line of scrimmage.

In the locker room, Thomas' presence was known, though he wasn't a rant-and-rave type of player.

"Joe was a quiet leader," his pal and teammate Ben Strickland said. "You know, he didn't want to be a hoo-rah-rah vocal guy. But when he said something, it mattered. And I think that was just his approach. You know, he was a fiery competitor, and most of the time it was (more) between his ears than vocally."

And after starting two dozen games for the Badgers — approximately 1,500 plays — over two years, Thomas was named second-team All-American by the Walter Camp Foundation and SI.com. But the highs brought on by a winning season, a bowl bid, first-round draft predictions and All-American honors would be tempered at the start of 2006.

10

DOWN, BUT NOT OUT

2006

On Jan. 2, 2006, Wisconsin faced Auburn in the Capital One Bowl in Orlando. The big news going into the game: It would be Barry Alvarez's final game as head coach of the Badgers before retiring. The transition would be smooth, to one of his assistants, Bret Bielema. But what happened in the third quarter would overshadow news about the coaches.

Joe Thomas had not lined up on defense in a game since he played defensive end in the 2003 Music City Bowl against Auburn.

He was considering entering the upcoming NFL draft, a year early. Would this added assignment be a risk?

"I volunteered," Thomas recalled. "I was super excited about it because my freshman year, I played defensive end in the bowl game I started. Because at that time, we had had a bunch of injuries on defense. And Auburn had a huge offensive line, and all they did was run the ball."* During bowl practice Thomas had heard the Badgers needed a bit more size at defensive end.

"I loved playing defense. So fun going after the quarterback," he said.

"So then junior year, we've got a nice big window before the bowl game. And I was always kind of joking with (the coaches) like,

---

* Auburn had offensive lineman Marcus McNeill and running backs Cadillac Williams and Ronnie Brown. All three would play at least six seasons in the NFL.

'Hey, whenever you're ready, I'm ready to play some more defense.' They felt like there was enough time to teach me defense. And so then they kind of agreed, after I sort of twisted their arm a little bit about it, to put me over there. And so I spent the whole week practicing defensive end. So it really was my idea. They co-signed it."

He had played three snaps at left end in a goal-line defense. He re-entered the game on the fifth play of Auburn's subsequent series. On the next play, he was in hot pursuit of Tigers tailback Kenny Irons.*

"I was running and I was on the back side of the play," Thomas recalled. "I turned, and I was trying to pursue to get in on the tackle. He cut back, and I was running as fast as I could. Not being a defensive player, I was running probably faster than my body could allow it, now 305 pounds. And so I stuck my foot in the ground and tried to turn and slow down at the same time. And it popped. I took one more step, and then I just fell. And as soon as I hit the ground, I knew what happened because I felt it, I heard it. I lost control of my knee and then you know, the fear sort of sets in right away. You're like, 'Oh crap, how bad is this?'"

Joe Panos, Thomas' friend and football mentor, a volunteer coach at Brookfield Central when Thomas was in school and a former Badger who had played in the NFL, saw it happen.

"I saw him run and I saw him fall," he told Tom Mulhern of the Wisconsin State Journal. "My heart hit the floor. I was numb. I had a sick feeling. I almost threw up. I knew exactly what happened. I grabbed the (doctor) and said, 'Joe's down, Joe's down!' I was the second one to know, aside from him. . . . We sat down on the sidelines. I looked at him and said, 'Listen, everything in life happens for a reason. It's an old saying. It's way cliché. But I'm a true, firm

---

* The moment would serve as a harbinger that would, in a way, connect Kenny Irons and Thomas. Irons would be drafted in the second round by the Cincinnati Bengals in 2007, the same year the Cleveland Browns took Thomas. Irons was the 49th player selected overall. In the Bengals' first exhibition game, Irons carried four times for 17 yards against Detroit. But in the second quarter, after trying to juke on a run, his left foot stuck in the turf. Diagnosis: A torn ACL. At first the Bengals were optimistic about his eventual return. But he never played a regular-season game.

believer. We've just got to find out what that reason is and we've got to find it through the journey of rehab and getting yourself back.'"

What is clear in Thomas' memory is the reaction immediately after he went down.

"One of the things that I do remember that was big in that moment — it's very stark to me — is being in the training room after my parents came in," Thomas said. "We're talking to the doctors, and they were explaining to me, 'You tore your ACL.' And the defensive line coach came in. John Palermo was one of the toughest guys I've ever been around. He was a hard, old-school-like, military-type general. He used the F-word every other word. And he was just the most grizzled guy ever. I remember him coming into the training room, and he just started crying. He said, 'I'm so sorry we did this to you, I'm so sorry, we never should have put you out on defense.' And at that moment, I was like: 'Am I dead? Holy cow, this is horrible.'"

It was Panos who was quick to offer encouragement and to show faith.

"I wanted to reassure him that all is going to be well, and nothing has changed as far as the type of football player that he has a chance to become next year," Panos told Mike Lucas of The Capital Times. "Basically, I care about the kid and I wanted to make sure he was all right and if he had any questions I could answer. I've had a lot of injuries during my (NFL) career and I didn't want him sitting there by himself."

Eric Vanden Heuvel, a quiet 340-pound freshman, stepped in at left tackle and Wisconsin went on to win, 24-10.

Thomas limped off on crutches, his 6-8, 305-pound frame hobbled by the injured right knee. Thomas' injury clouded Alvarez's coaching finale. "That just makes you sick when something like that happens," Alvarez told the Associated Press.

In the aftermath, Thomas kept his head up. He knew he had been projected as a first-round pick. "There's no doubt in my mind that I'll have plenty of information, have a full scope of where I'm able to go and how things will turn out," he said at the time.

One thing was certain: Thomas was headed for surgery and rehabilitation.

Knee injuries are common in sports that require strength, speed and quick changes of direction. They can happen a number of ways — on a sharp cutback on a field or even in non-contact moments.

The letters "ACL" in the sports pages have made even the most casual of fans take note. The anterior cruciate ligament is in the middle of the knee, as opposed to the medial collateral ligament, which is on the inside, and the lateral collateral ligament on the outside. "Cruciate" is Latin — cruciatus, from crux, meaning "cross." The ACL is a band of tissue that connects bones and cartilage and stops the tibia (shin) from sliding in front of the femur (thigh) bone. While we often hear about ACLs in football, females tend to tear them more than males.

Recovery time from a torn ACL varies but has greatly improved over the years with medical advancements. Years ago, players might miss a season or have their career shortened. By 2006, athletes were able to return to action sometimes within a season. Who knows how some notable careers shortened by a knee injury might have been different with today's medical techniques? In 1951, Mickey Mantle tore his ACL, MCL and meniscus simultaneously when his foot caught in a drain grate in Yankee Stadium. In 1968, Chicago Bears running back Gale Sayers tore up his knee similarly on one play. Both are in the Hall of Fame for their respective sports, yet could they have gone on to even greater achievements? Compare them to later examples, such as Willis McGahee of the University of Miami, who tore anterior, posterior and medial ligaments in the 2003 National Championship game, yet still went on to play more than a decade in the NFL. His teammate Frank Gore tore an ACL in college yet went on to become the NFL's third leading all-time rusher. Publicly, Thomas shrugged off the injury. "I'm not worried about it," he told Jim Polzin of Capital Newspapers. But serious injuries will emotionally tax any athlete. Few athletes can fend off those slight droplets of doubt from creeping in.

The physical post-surgery process can be a solitary one. It takes place after the cameras go away, after the initial news stories run their course. The first few weeks, Thomas said, is spent with limited activity and plenty of icing and elevation, while trying to regain range of motion and balance.

When the NFL Pro Timing Day rolled around on March 8, 2006, Thomas wasn't there. It didn't appear to faze him not to show up at the evaluation for athletes that is considered less extensive than the combine, held in multiple places, and offers a chance for more interaction than the combine.

"Being able to have one more year where I don't have to worry about it is kind of nice," he told the Wisconsin State Journal.

Instead, Thomas was already looking forward to the season opener in September against Bowling Green. And meanwhile, he and his dad were planning a canoe trip in May to Quetico Provincial Park, about 650 miles away in Ontario. "It's given me a lot of time to do some things I normally am not able to do," he said. "I've been able to do some things in the offseason to be able to enjoy it. I've been able to study a little bit harder, dedicate some more time to my friends, and plan a few fishing trips. So, all is not lost."

His father didn't seem too worried, either.

"He's a goal-oriented person," Eric Thomas told the Wisconsin State Journal.

Over time, draft predictions of Thomas landing within the first 15 picks actually improved. Draft guru Mel Kiper Jr. forecasted Thomas would be taken within the first three picks. That would turn out to be a prescient observation.

Still, Thomas was facing reality of coming back from a serious injury. "I was pretty down," he told Lucas of The Capital Times. "And it was hard to face the facts. Joe (Panos) was there supporting me and telling me, 'You're not going to miss a snap next season. You'll be ready by the start of training camp.' I really had no idea about the injury as far as rehabbing. You always think the worst-case scenario when something like this happens. And I thought my football career was over."

Thomas did his homework. He talked with former Wisconsin and NFL players. He kept after rehab.

Just a little more than four months after his ACL surgery, Thomas was being projected as high as second in the draft, according to Kiper and Scouts Inc. Draftscout.com had him third. (All three forecasts had Brady Quinn going ahead of Thomas.)

Panos stayed optimistic. "I will bet my last dollar that Joe Thomas is going to become a better person and a better football player because of this," he told Mulhern.

That prophecy would come true.

Milwaukee Journal Sentinel sportswriter Jeff Potrykus, in his 2020 compilation of the greatest Wisconsin players over the previous 25 years, ranked Thomas at No. 2, behind running back Ron Dayne (the 1999 Heisman Trophy winner). He lauded Thomas's on-field achievements but said "The most enduring image, however, was seeing Thomas running the Camp Randall Stadium steps in April 2006, a little more than three months after he suffered a torn ACL while playing defense in the Capital One Bowl."

As the 2006 season approached, new Badgers head coach Bret Bielema was taking the reins of a team that was poised for a breakout year. Joe Thomas was entering his final year wearing Wisconsin's red and white. And the NFL loomed on the horizon.

It would be a year of excitement and accomplishments — and tragedy.

11

SENIOR YEAR: STARTING ON A WINNING NOTE

2006-07

Joe Thomas' senior season with Wisconsin would be tumultuous and triumphant.

Seven months after his injury, Thomas felt comfortable to play and awaited a doctor's OK.

He would be one of only two returning starters on the offensive line, along with Kraig Urbik (who had switched on the right side from tackle to guard).*

The media also awaited Thomas' return: He was named to the Sporting News preseason All-America first team.

Thomas was one of Wisconsin's representatives at the NCAA's media day in Chicago. The annual event serves to hype the upcoming season and was an opportunity for sportswriters to get to know players, talk to coaches and hear about expectations. The interviews and access provide fodder for journalists: Writers could fill a notebook worth of stories, while broadcast media could gain background and perspective to use when calling games.

The highlight for Thomas, though, was heading to Wrigley Field

---

* What's in the water? Urbik, the only other returning offensive lineman with Thomas, graduated in 2004 from Hudson High School, located on the St. Croix River on the outskirts of Minneapolis in western Wisconsin. Eric Vanden Heuvel, Thomas' replacement in the bowl game after the knee injury, is a 2005 Hudson High graduate. And Annie Nelson, who would become Annie Thomas, graduated from Hudson in 2002, the year she helped lead the basketball team to a state title over Waukesha South, 65-46. She led all scorers with 17 points in the game.

with other Wisconsin folks for a Chicago Cubs game. "It was so hot, we made it through about an inning and a half," he said. "And we're just sitting in the cheap seats. We said, 'Screw this.' And so we went to Wrigleyville, drinking beer and watching the rest of the game from the bar to escape the heat."*

For a long time, offensive linemen rarely received their due from the media or from fans. But by the time Thomas was playing that had changed, thanks in large part to increased scrutiny — additional camera angles, more media analyses and closer attention from hardcore football diehards. It became routine for Thomas to be the focus of newspaper stories — such as Tom Mulhern's four-word lead in an Aug. 26, 2006, Wisconsin State Journal piece, "Joe Thomas is back."

Thomas had put in a lot of hard work over a long time during recovery, and he was feeling confident. But he knew the real test would be the first time he wore pads in practice. That day came in August 2006 when he lined up against reserve tight end Matt Brown. After that initial clash at the line, Thomas knew he was OK.

"He hit me and I said, 'My knee is OK. I can take this,'" he told Mulhern. "It's that first hit, it's that first time you're sprinting out and blocking a corner, you have to cut on it . . . Once you get that over with, it's all easy from there."

A day before Wisconsin's season opener, the Wausau Daily Herald quoted Nolan Nawrocki, an NFL draft analyst for Pro Football Weekly, as saying, "Thomas has the feet of a ballerina and he is huge and massive. The best athletes are always at left tackle and some of them have been converted tight ends or defensive ends. Thomas has those positions in his history."

As Thomas' confidence was growing, so was interest in the Outland Award.

Named for Dr. John Outland, a 19th-century football star who later coached, the award has since 1946 been bestowed on the best interior lineman in the country. That first year, football writers

---

* Thomas wasn't wimping out. The high during media day in Chicago was 100 degrees.

voted George Connor of Notre Dame as best interior lineman. Connor was the only winner of the award who Outland lived to see; he died the following year. Each year, the writers consider a list of 20 players from the pool of linemen in the country. The award would be presented after the season.

Thomas, before the Badgers had taken a snap in Camp Randall for his senior year, had been named a semifinalist.

He had also landed on multiple preseason All-America lists: Playboy, Lindy's, Street & Smith's and Athlon's all had him as among the nation's best players.

Head coach Bret Bielema lauded Thomas at the start of the season. He didn't tout him for the Heisman Trophy — it would be highly unusual for an offensive lineman to win that award — but extolled what Thomas brought to the team.

"There are things that I think Joe brings to the table that I think set him apart," Bielema told Jim Polzin of The Capital Times. "I find it interesting to hear commentators talk about who's going to win the Heisman or what person is going to be the one that takes the grandest prize of them all. And I think the definition that anybody kind of gets out of it is the Heisman Trophy is supposed to go to the person that performs at the highest level and brings his team to a higher level of success because of what he does."*

Shortly before the Badgers played their first game of Thomas' senior year, Wisconsin's Athletics Department unveiled a website promoting Thomas for awards like the Outland and Lombardi. The department planned to update the site with videos and features focusing on Thomas both on and off the field. It showed Thomas fishing, wearing a floppy hat and sunglasses, and in his offseason summer internship with Merrill Lynch.

Clearly the intention was to humanize a player who fans might not even recognize when he wasn't wearing a helmet. At the time,

---

* For the record, Ohio State quarterback Troy Smith won the 2006 Heisman easily, with running back Darren McFadden of Arkansas a distant second. Finishing third was a name who would continue to be linked with Thomas in a number of ways: Notre Dame quarterback Brady Quinn.

social media was in its infancy, yet colleges had for years been using promotional brochures and other public-relations tools to tout players for awards.

Thomas was named a captain for his senior year, along with quarterback John Stocco and linebacker Mark Zalewski.

The Badgers hit the road for their opener against Bowling Green at a neutral site: Cleveland Browns Stadium.

While a nonconference game might be considered a simple tune-up for Wisconsin, it served as an important personal test for Thomas, and he passed. "My knee felt great the whole game. I never once felt I was limping around or favoring it at all. Everything I did out there as far as my knee was concerned was 100 percent. The next step for me was just playing a game," he said.

Wisconsin won, 35-14. By All-American standards, Thomas didn't have a stellar game. In the opener, poor footwork allowed senior defensive end Devon Parks to get past him for an 11-yard sack. Thomas also was called for holding against Parks. In fairness, Parks was no slouch; he would be named co-MVP on Bowling Green's team that year and go on to a stint in Arena Football.

A week later at home, Wisconsin toppled Western Illinois, 34-10, at Camp Randall, and continued fattening up with a 14-0 win over San Diego State. Then the real test would come: Michigan in week 4.

As the Michigan game neared, talk wasn't on the usual star position players but rather the lines of each team — the Badgers' offensive front vs. the Wolverines' defense, which included another matchup with LaMarr Woodley.

Both teams were 3-0, and it was the Big Ten opener for both schools. Michigan's run defense was the nation's best, allowing a measly 20 yards a game. They had sacked quarterbacks 13 times in three games. The Wolverines entered the game a 14-point favorite. Wisconsin offensive line coach Bob Palcic told Mulhern, "We have our hands full."

For Thomas' 29th start at left tackle, he relied on something that served as a theme in his life.

"If you're prepared and you know what you're doing, you can

go into the game and you know exactly what you're seeing," he told Polzin. "You go out and you play football and you don't get enamored with a big crowd or being at Michigan or great names you're playing against."

In the end, Michigan handed Wisconsin a 27-13 loss, and the Wolverines' defense lived up to its billing, holding the Badgers to 12 yards of offense. Speaking as a team member in postgame interviews, Thomas said the Badgers had known they would face adversity and how they needed to respond better in the future. Individually, he played a great game against a great player in Woodley — and performed so well that the Wisconsin coaches named him offensive player of the game.*

Privately, Thomas admitted harboring some negative motivation.

"I hated playing Michigan," he recalls. "I think it went back to being offended that they didn't recruit me, and then I kind of wanted to maybe go there potentially at least. I liked the opportunity maybe to have a chance to go visit. So when we had a chance to kind of stick it to 'em, it was like 'Hey, see what you're missing?'"

His performance in the game showed something else.

"[Woodley] was probably the best opponent I played against my senior year," Thomas said. "And I played well. That was a moment where a lot of teams and scouts said, 'Well, after you did that, we could tell that your knee is healthy,' and that helped my draft stock."

On Saturday, Sept. 30, the Badgers took their 3-1 record to Bloomington, Indiana. The Hoosiers were 2-2 and hosting their Big Ten opener. They were on the way to a 5-7 record while their coach, Jerry Hoeppner, dealt with surgery for a brain tumor. (He died fewer than nine months later.)

Wisconsin rebounded from the Michigan loss and trounced

---

* How good was Woodley? In his junior and senior seasons at Michigan, he racked up 84 tackles — most of them solo—and 18 sacks. In the 2007 NFL draft, Woodley went in the second round, 46th overall, to Pittsburgh. Woodley would go on to play 110 games in the NFL — more than any of the four players at his position drafted ahead of him in the first round.

Indiana, 52-17. It would be the most points the Badgers scored in a game all season. Stocco threw for 304 yards. P.J. Hill rushed for 129 yards and three touchdowns. The Badgers were now 4-1. They would begin to prepare for a weak Northwestern team at home. There was a lot to be joyful about in the lockers after the game.

That joy would be short-lived for Thomas.

12

LOSING A FRIEND

They were a tight quartet of high school friends whose common bond was sports: Joe Thomas, Ben Strickland, Steve Johnson and Luke Homan. Homan had been Thomas' first "agent" when he had had the foresight years earlier to craft a contract saying as much when they were kids.

It was Homan's dad who had assembled a basketball team for tournament play from the more talented kids in Brookfield, and the four boys eventually came together on the court.

Strickland and Johnson would play football as walk-ons at Wisconsin with Thomas. Homan was a two-sport star in high school. He played quarterback and kicker on the Brookfield Central High School Lancers' 2002 state final football team. In basketball, he competed in three state tournaments and was a starter on teams that reached the finals in Madison in 2002 and 2003.

"We were really probably the closest out of the four of us," Thomas said of Homan. "Ben and Steve were backdoor neighbors. So they grew up since the third or fourth grade. And then Luke and I were super close, because we started playing basketball together by around fourth grade. So I think we kind of started playing together first. And then we started playing baseball together, around the track team together. A lot of times, I would travel with his family to basketball tournaments. His dad was a coach. He was an only child. And if my parents couldn't go, I'd just ride along with them, stay in the hotel room with them. Part of the reason we became so close is because his parents were like a second set of mom and dad for me. And he was our quarterback on the football team. I was a tight end and, of course, his favorite target."

On the basketball court, as a 6-foot-3 guard with great range, Homan averaged 18.6 points, 5.3 rebounds and four assists per game as a senior. The Milwaukee Journal Sentinel named him first-team all-area and honorable mention all-state that year.

Homan started his college career at University of Wisconsin-Milwaukee in 2005-06, playing for Bruce Pearl. Like his pals Strickland and Johnson, he was a walk-on. But a combination of little playing time during his first two seasons and Pearl's departure to Tennessee made Homan rethink his dream of playing at the Division I level. He transferred to Division III UW-La Crosse, where he was a reserve on the team while majoring in finance.

La Crosse, a narrow city of about 50,000 people, is on the Wisconsin-Minnesota border, along the Mississippi River, the dividing line between the states.

Homan was celebrating Oktoberfest, a well-known party throughout the city's bars, in the early morning hours of Sept. 30, 2006. The following morning, his roommates had not seen him, and he did not show up for a golf outing.

The police were notified, and they investigated and used search dogs, looking on land and in the river. They posted signs for clues. They learned early on that Homan had been drinking at several bars, late. They traced his whereabouts to several specific downtown bars, but the trail ended at Riverside Park. Horse-mounted units and dive-team members were brought in. UW-La Crosse athletes immediately posted "missing person" fliers.

Steve Johnson said that he, Thomas and Strickland heard the news about Homan being missing after the Indiana game. When they learned that Homan still hadn't turned up, the three asked for, and received, permission from Wisconsin coach Bret Bielema to make the 140-mile drive to La Crosse to aid in the search.

"I remember that car ride," Strickland said. "From Madison to La Crosse is about a two-hour drive, but we didn't talk the whole way up. Just being in the car felt like forever. But I felt fortunate to have Joe and Steve there for me — two of my guys that I see as brothers. We didn't have to say anything to each other; we're there for each other."

Mark Adams, the Brookfield Central boys basketball coach, knew his four former players well. He also traveled to La Crosse to help in the search.

"I don't know if anybody would say one was a best friend more than another, but Luke and Joe had something there," he said. "They were pretty tight."

On Oct. 2, 2006, Adams was standing next to the police chaplain, watching the boats chug up and down the river until they stopped suddenly. Divers went in, and Adams saw them pull up Homan's body.

"I sat there and cried for quite a while," Johnson told Brett Christopherson of The Post-Crescent. "Joe was with me. Ben was actually by the river. It was a pretty emotional day. It's going to be tough to make it through."

"When he turned up in the river. . . . those guys were devastated," Adams said. "I mean, that was really an awakening. I remember going up to all three of those guys before I was getting ready to leave to drive back to Brookfield and I said, 'Hey, whatever happens to you guys — I'm not going to tell you how to run your life, but if you guys go out anywhere along the way with your buddies, and you're going to any area where you're going to bars or anything like that, don't ever leave one another, you know? Don't ever leave one another because somehow — and I'm not blaming anybody — but somehow Luke got alone. He was lost track of and then this was the end result. And they said, 'Yeah, coach, we appreciate that.'"

The park had no railing, just a small curb a few inches high along the river's edge. Water temperature at that point would have been in the mid-50s to the mid-60s, records show. Anne Aldrich-Abraham, a newspaper reporter who covered the Homan case thoroughly for about a year, said: "The downtown is close to the river. If you're drunk, when it's dark and you're in the river alone, you won't survive."

Police reported that there were no signs of trauma on Homan's body. The police chief blamed binge drinking.

Homan's death would turn out to be a catalyst for change in the river city's alcohol culture. The tragedy also brought an outpouring of support for a likeable young man.

Homan was, by many accounts, a good kid who loved country music, a loyal friend, and son to parents Jerry and Patti.

Homan's basketball coach at UW-La Crosse, Ken Koelbl, said in the La Crosse Tribune. "He was just a tremendous breath of fresh air" for the basketball program, calling him "a great role model on our team, for all our players."

"You couldn't ask for a better kid," Jerry Homan told Kate Schott of the La Crosse Tribune.

Thomas remembers the bond with basketball between son and father. "It was just a terrible situation all around," he said.

Strickland told Mike Lucas of The Capital Times, "Luke was the guy who told me to chase my dreams and always dream big."

A memorial for Homan was installed near the park, close to where his body was found. A basketball hoop and other tributes were left, including his No. 40 written on a cross.

The funeral was set for Oct. 5 at St. John Vianney Catholic Church in Brookfield, directly across the street from the high school. Thomas, Strickland and Johnson were pallbearers. Tennessee basketball coach Bruce Pearl, who had coached Homan at UW-Milwaukee, attended the funeral.

Unfortunately, two lingering repercussions hung over the tragedy.

First, compounding the grief for friends and family was the emergence of a strange rumor and speculation about a possible serial killer in the area. Within a 10-year period, seven young men had died in the river in the same area. Most of the deaths had involved alcohol, though, and the connections were tenuous at best: Young white males in a similar vicinity. Police stood fast that Homan's death was solely an alcohol-related accident.

Also, during their investigation, police had arrested and cited a La Crosse student for underage drinking the same night Homan died. He had told police it was possible that he and Homan were in the park and that his best guess was that Homan tripped, but he could not remember. Almost a year later, he pleaded no contest to two misdemeanor counts of obstructing officers. He was sentenced to 48 hours in jail and a year of probation. A district attorney on the case said in court the suspect "threw a cloud" over the investigation into Homan's death "that will remain probably forever."

Homan's death left a void among loving parents and close friends. But it brought people together to finally address safety concerns.

As an Associated Press story weeks after Homan's death stated, "La Crosse officials have debated for years how to keep drunken students safe, but some say there may be no answer for a town with three colleges, three rivers and $3 pitchers of beer."

Banning late-night drink specials was discussed, as was potential fines for bar owners who served drunken patrons. Students started Operation: River Watch. Volunteers patrolled the riverside late night Thursdays through Saturdays. One police officer was quoted saying: "It's the first time I can remember that you actually have students and the department working together toward the same goal. It's been amazing." A $33,000 project to construct preventive barriers drew mixed reviews. The city adopted a public intoxication ordinance and spent about $60,000 on railings for the park.

In August 2007, almost a year after Homan's death, the FBI issued its ruling: There was no foul play in the deaths of the college-age men who had drowned in the river over 10 years.

In 2007, the Luke Homan Memorial Tournament was established at Brookfield Central High School. The basketball tournament is still held.

To this day, when Johnson reflects on this time in his life, he remembers Bielema's immediate reaction when the three asked for permission to leave campus to go to La Crosse. "He was — you know, the cliché term is a 'player's coach' — but you knew that he legitimately cared about all of his players. With Luke, there was nothing that was Wisconsin Badgers first or Coach B first or your teammates first. It was very much 'Go take care of your family, take care of yourself, take care of your friends.'"

Bielema is a former lineman who played at the University of Iowa. While he's in control on the field, he has a gregarious personality. He's the type of guy you would find bellied up to a bar to shoot the breeze about the game on television, or your uncle lounging on a patio in a back yard. Bielema's response was shaped by his own personal tragedy.

"When I was in college, my sophomore year, I lost my sister. And when I was going through the funeral service of my sister, I was in uncontrollable hysterics, crying, and my pastor grabbed me. And he said, 'Bret, I know it doesn't make sense now. But at some point in the future, your life, the passing of your sister will have a cause and will have a reason and it'll be very clear to you when this happens.' You know, I'm 19 years old, and I'm looking at this guy, and I don't know what he's saying, right? And I'm telling you, when I walked into that meeting with those three young men who were in the most distraught moment of their lives, that's when I knew everything had a purpose. And so I was able to relate and give them thoughts about how I handled the moment. We talked about different things. I let them have as much time as they needed to grieve."

Bielema left it up to his three athletes to decide whether they would play against Northwestern.

"It was just a very tough moment, but one that I'll always remember because in its own unique way it allowed me to heal as well," he said.

Thomas, Strickland and Johnson, in the throes of grief, returned to Wisconsin as the Badgers prepared to play Northwestern. Thomas admitted afterward to reporters that it was difficult to get ready for that game, after practicing just one day that week.

"I've never had so much on my mind, and I've never thought so little about the game," he told Brett Christopherson of the Appleton

Joe Thomas in 2016. It would be his 10th straight season starting all 16 games and his 10th straight year being named to the Pro Bowl. *(Joshua Gunter, cleveland.com)*

Joe took to sports — all sports — early in life. He wasn't a star right away, but competition was in his blood. He also became an avid and lifelong outdoorsman. *(Courtesy of Sally Thomas)*

"At 2 or 3, he was able to hold a rod. So I'd bring him along," Joe's father, Eric Thomas, said. "He truly enjoyed it." *(Courtesy of Sally Thomas)*

One of the first organized teams Joe (No. 13) played on, the Brookfield Magic did well in tournaments, in part because they had played together for a while and developed chemistry. *(Courtesy of Sally Thomas)*

Joe started playing football in seventh grade. He played so many positions in high school that he kept various extra jerseys with position-eligible numbers on the sideline, ready to change into. *(Courtesy of Sally Thomas)*

The four childhood pals bonded early through sports and played together on the Brookfield Central High School football team. Left to right: Luke Homan, Ben Strickland, Steve Johnson and Joe Thomas. *(Courtesy of Joe Thomas)*

Joe Thomas and Steve Marcelle by the shot put leaderboard at a high school track meet. Marcelle was a sophomore at another school when he reached out for advice from Thomas, who gladly obliged despite the fact they would compete against one another. Marcelle went on to compete at Georgia Tech. *(Courtesy of Steve Marcelle)*

Thomas started at left tackle for Wisconsin as a sophomore in 2004. "He's probably the most athletic lineman we've had," head coach Barry Alvarez told the media before the season. *(David Stluka)*

In Thomas' senior year, the Badgers defeated rival Minnesota to claim the traditional trophy, Paul Bunyan's Axe. Here, he wields it for the crowd at Camp Randall Stadium. *(David Stluka)*

Thomas answers questions in Berea on April 29, 2007, a day after the Browns picked the offensive lineman with the No. 3 overall pick in the draft. "You can't just have a great quarterback and no line, because if you don't have anybody to protect him, he's not going to be a great quarterback," Thomas said. *(Lynn Ischay, The Plain Dealer)*

Thomas rallies the crowd at the Browns-Jets game in 2007, his rookie season. "I learned real fast what going against an elite NFL pass rusher was like," Thomas says of his first year. "We faced a gauntlet of top tier pass rushers" including James Harrison, Justin Smith, Mario Williams and Jason Taylor. But after a few games, he realized, "I can do this." *(John Kuntz, cleveland.com)*

Thomas signs autographs for fans after Browns training camp, August 2008. (*Scott Shaw, The Plain Dealer*)

Brady Quinn and Thomas answer reporters' questions at the Browns practice facility in Berea on Dec. 29, 2008. The team that day fired General Manager Phil Savage and head coach Romeo Crennel. Thomas and Quinn were first-round draft choices in 2007. Crennel was their first head coach in the NFL. (*Chuck Crow, The Plain Dealer*)

Thomas and fellow offensive linemen Eric Steinbach (65) and Alex Mack (55) take a break during practice in 2011 in Berea. *(Chuck Crow, The Plain Dealer)*

Thomas sets up a block for Trent Richardson during a game against the Oakland Raiders in 2012. *(Joshua Gunter, cleveland.com)*

Thomas blocked for a league-record 20 quarterbacks during his career in Cleveland. Shown here are (at top, with Thomas in 2017) DeShone Kizer, Kevin Hogan and Cody Kessler, and (bottom, in 2015) Austin Davis, Josh McCown and Johnny Manziel. *(John Kuntz, cleveland.com)*

Thomas picks up a fumble after Brandon Weeden was sacked in a 2013 game against the Buffalo Bills. He gained a few yards on the play — a rare treat for a lineman. The Browns won 37-24. *(Chuck Crow, The Plain Dealer)*

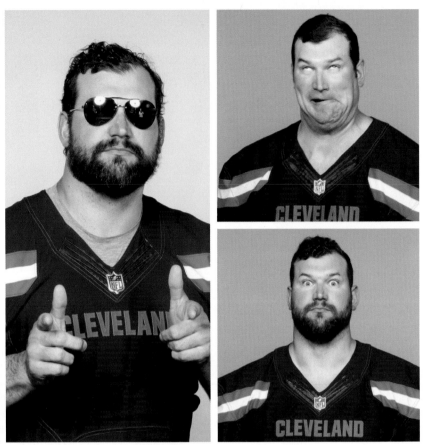

Thomas didn't take himself too seriously during Browns' media day.
(Cleveland Browns)

Thomas collaborated with Great Lakes Brewing Co. on a special brew: 73 Kolsch.
(Marc Bona, cleveland.com)

Thomas, right, soaks in a pool filled with ice water along with teammates during training camp in July 2017, in Berea. (*John Kuntz, cleveland.com*)

On his 10,000th consecutive snap, Thomas opened a hole for running back Isaiah Crowell during a 2017 game in Baltimore. (*John Kuntz, cleveland.com*)

Thomas leaves the field after suffering what would be a career-ending triceps injury against Tennessee on Oct. 22, 2017 in Cleveland. (*John Kuntz, cleveland.com*)

During his retirement announcement in 2018, Thomas poses for media with his wife, Annie, and children, from left, Camryn, Logan and Jack. *(John Kuntz, cleveland.com)*

Two Cleveland greats meet: LeBron James hugs Thomas during a timeout in a Cavaliers game in 2018. *(Joshua Gunter, cleveland.com)*

Browns greats greet Thomas as he is enshrined as a member of the
Browns Legends on Sept. 18, 2022. *(John Kuntz, cleveland.com)*

The Thomas family, from left: Reese, Annie, Logan, Camryn, Joe and Jack.
(Courtesy of Joe Thomas)

Post-Crescent. "As soon as that whistle blew, somehow, some way, I was able to go out there and know what was going on."

And in the game, Thomas felt his friend's presence.

"I got rolled up on the third play of the game, and I was hit so hard that I have a bruise on my leg," he told Christopherson. "I thought that was it for my knee. Somehow, I just stood up and walked away. The only way to explain that was that Luke was right there."

Wisconsin won that game, 41-9. Thomas and his offensive line mates held firm again, helping P.J. Hill rush for career highs — 35 carries for 249 yards and a touchdown.

Johnson never takes for granted the friendship he has with Thomas and Strickland, then and now — from knowing each other as kids, growing up together, playing together at Wisconsin and rooming together.

"I know I've said this to my parents, when I knew that we had buddies who were having a tough time with grieving. I got to grieve, Joe got to grieve, Ben got to grieve with their best friends."

That grief came to a head after the Northwestern game.

"That week was very much a blur, I would say," Johnson said. "Ben, Joe and I, we had a hot tub at our house. We had some beers, and we just cried. We sat in this hot tub. And we were able to just absolutely clear our plate of all the emotions. And there was a ton of tears. There was a ton of laughter. It was a ton of just having that unique opportunity to do that. I think it's incredible. There's no judgment, no nothing. We just sat in our back yard in this hot tub and just bawled our eyes out thinking about our buddy. So the Luke story doesn't finish for me without being able to do that.

"I know that we had friends who are not able to have what we were able to have in terms of Joe, Ben and I, in terms of our ability to lean on one another and get through your most difficult time, really I would say for all of us in our life at this point. I was unbelievably grateful for that ability to do that with good friends."

13

NFL IN SIGHT

On Tuesdays during his senior year, Thomas did not practice to allow rest for his rehabilitated knee. On those days, he became a de facto coach.

"When he sits out the Tuesday practices, he definitely becomes a great coach to us younger guys," said Eric Vanden Heuvel, who had replaced Thomas in the game when he was injured. And as the season wore on, Bielema routinely called on Thomas as one of the leaders on the team to guide younger players. That was a critical decision on Bielema's part, knowing he could trust Thomas and other seniors on a team that had 23 freshmen or sophomores on a two-deep depth chart.

On Oct. 14, Wisconsin manhandled rival Minnesota, 48-12. The Badgers had rebounded strongly since the loss to Michigan, scoring 141 points in the three games. The Minnesota game had a special twist: It's one of the many Big Ten games with creative traveling trophies, in this case Paul Bunyan's Axe. After the game, Thomas was one of the players who joyfully lugged the 6-foot-long, almost cartoonish axe onto the field.

Wins against Purdue, Illinois and Penn State followed. (Nittany Lions fans also had to endure seeing their coach, Joe Paterno, break his leg on the sideline after Wisconsin linebacker DeAndre Levy inadvertently barreled into him.)

Next, Wisconsin traveled west to face the Iowa Hawkeyes. Wisconsin had had a good run over the previous four years with its current class of seniors, with winning seasons and bowl-game appearances. But one thorn in their side had been the Hawkeyes, who had beaten them in each of their last four matchups. Bielema turned to his seniors to remind their teammates about the game's importance. He told the Associated Press that Thomas "didn't yell and go into rah-rah speech. He basically said that if someone needs that type of motivation to play the game of football, they're probably not going to be successful." Wisconsin won, 24-21.

The Badgers were 10-1 going into their final game. It was Joe Thomas' last game at Camp Randall. On senior day, as he was announced to the crowd, Thomas had tears in his eyes. The Badgers then breezed by Buffalo, 35-3.

"I remember celebrating after we played Buffalo," said Strickland, a junior at the time. "It wasn't a very competitive game, but just celebrating after the game and with something that all the seniors always did with anybody else who stayed out there after the game — the fifth quarter. And so I remember that, just enjoying playing together one last time at Camp Randall, and singing and dancing with the band, and you know, jumping all over each other."

That elation would continue in Madison. Leading up to the Capital One Bowl vs. Arkansas on Jan. 1, the National Scouting Combine released its NFL draft prospects listing Thomas at No. 3 (behind Brady Quinn at No. 1 and Clemson defensive end Gaines Adams at No. 2).

The American Football Coaches Association and Rivals.com also named Thomas first-team All-American.

But all of this — an 11-1 regular season, the accolades, the award — would take a back seat to an even more important moment.

Thomas had been dating Annie Nelson, a 6-1 forward for the Wisconsin women's basketball team. He initially planned to propose during a carriage ride in Central Park in New York on Dec. 4 — his 22nd birthday — but travel plans changed. Instead, Joe proposed on Dec. 6 on a boardwalk at Walt Disney World. The following night, he received the Outland Award at a ceremony in

Orlando. Thomas was the third Big Ten lineman in four years to win the award.*

Life was busy for Joe Thomas: He was newly engaged, a final college bowl game was coming up and the NFL was on the horizon.

Teammates reported that Thomas never talked about the various predictions putting him in the upper echelon of potential NFL draft spots. "He'll do anything for the team," teammate Mark Zalewski told Jacey Zembal of the Wausau Daily Herald. "He just wants to be the best. . . . He has said in interviews that he wants to be remembered as the hardest working player who has ever come through here. That mentality with the ability he has is why he is so special."**

Thomas would have one more opportunity to show off that talent while wearing the Badgers' red and white.

January 1 is a college football fan's dream day. The 2007 lineup included six games, meaning college football would be on television for more than 12 continuous hours across four networks.***

In the Capital One Bowl, Wisconsin faced a slightly favored Arkansas team that played with five defensive linemen, forcing the Badgers' linemen into an especially physical contest.

"They had five big, fat guys stacked on all of our five fat guys,"

---

* Thomas being named Outland Award winner carries an odd footnote. Michigan's Jake Long was named Big Ten offensive lineman of the year in 2006 and 2007. While Long would go on to a fine NFL career (he was the No. 1 overall pick in 2008), it remains a bit puzzling as to how Thomas could be named the best among his peers on both sides of the ball in the country but not in his conference.

** The Capital One Bowl on Jan. 1, 2007, was the second time in school history Wisconsin faced Arkansas. On Nov. 9, 1912, the Badgers routed the Razorbacks, 64-7. Wisconsin went 7-0 that year with four shutouts and allowed only 29 points. The Arkansas coach, Hugo Bezdek, is responsible for the school's "Razorbacks" nickname. He would later become the inaugural head coach of the Cleveland Rams. Also, as the perpetual coaching carousel turned, Bielema would wind up as head coach at Arkansas from 2013 through 2017.

*** Two days after the Capital One Bowl, LSU faced Notre Dame in the Sugar Bowl — notable because the two quarterbacks in the game were JaMarcus Russell and Brady Quinn. It was Russell who had the better game, completing 21 of 34 passes for 332 yards in a 41-14 rout. Three months later both would be drafted in the first round, with Russell the No. 1 overall selection.

Thomas told Tom Mulhern of the Wisconsin State Journal. The pressure worked. Wisconsin quarterback John Stocco was sacked six times. (None of those sacks could be attributed directly to Thomas.) Yet the Badgers' offense rose in the final four-plus minutes, eating clock and preserving a slim lead. They won, 17-14.

The Wisconsin teams on which Joe Thomas played had a combined record of 38-13.* Thomas would leave Wisconsin with his head high.

Weeks later, the Senior Bowl was held in Mobile, Alabama. Thomas was invited but chose not to play. With every NFL draft forecast projecting Thomas to go high in the first round, the exhibition game served only as a chance for injury, not to move up in the projections.

As Thomas approached the end of his time in college, the NFL combine behind him and an agent signed, he and Bielema hit the speak-and-sign circuit — sports banquets and a tailgate party at an automotive dealership. Thomas recalls it as a fun time, filled with anticipation of his wedding and the draft. He also was named one of two recipients from the University of Wisconsin of the Big Ten Medal of Honor, along with decorated Canadian hockey player Sara Bauer.** The award honors athletes in the conference who excel at scholarship and athletics.

College, of course, had not been just football (and sometimes discus). Thomas had studied business, emphasizing real estate and urban land economics. He had also served a summer internship with Merrill Lynch in Madison. "Even if I am able to have a successful career in the NFL, I'd still like to do real estate after that," he told Aaron Brenner in The Badger Herald.

Thomas's 3.5 grade-point average wasn't earned on the proverbial easy-athlete curriculum. A Sports Illustrated profile written by veteran sportswriter Peter King right before the draft said, "There

---

* Compare the 38 wins in four years at Wisconsin with Thomas' time in Cleveland. The Browns won 48 games in the 11 seasons he played. Wisconsin went to four bowl games, winning two. The Browns did not make the postseason during Thomas' time in the NFL.

** Bauer might not be a household name outside of women's hockey, but in four years at Wisconsin, the 5-3 forward led her teams to an astounding 125-20-9 record.

may not be a better school in America to study real estate and urban land economics than Wisconsin," citing U.S. News & World Report's rankings. (It remains one of the best in the country.) And while Thomas could have lapsed into full senior-slump blow-off mode, his final-semester classes were Finance 300, real estate finance, business law and real estate development.

Thomas' legacy at Wisconsin was shaped primarily by his play on the field, but it was done in a position that most of the time, to most fans, is invisible.

There is a story, probably apocryphal, about Albert Einstein. He supposedly once wrote 10 basic equations on a chalkboard: $9x1=9$, $9x2=18$, and so on. But the final one — $9x10=91$ — was obviously incorrect. Students mocked him. He then turned to the class and pointed out that they had noticed only the one mistake; they had ignored the first nine successes. That story might serve as an analogy for offensive linemen. They aren't noticed until that yellow flag is thrown, an official makes the symbol for a holding infraction, and the lineman is seen standing sheepishly or trudging back to the huddle. That's the kind of attention offensive linemen usually get.

During his college years, media coverage given to Thomas was interesting. Usually the so-called "skill position" players like quarterbacks, running backs and receivers gain more attention, in part because their play is easily quantified statistically. We all know a running back who can go for 100 yards has had a good game, or a quarterback who throws for 300-plus yards with more touchdowns than interceptions is excelling. But offensive linemen? You have to analyze tapes to see holes open and quarterbacks find a split-second more time to throw to evaluate them. But comb through coverage of Thomas in college, and you will find volumes of stories, with coaches and others willing to talk about how great he was.

"Joe's one of the most level-headed guys I know," Badgers' center Marcus Coleman told Brenner. "If you didn't know him, you would never expect he was an All-American football player."

The Capital Times' Mike Lucas, who covered Thomas extensively, said Badgers fans respected Thomas. "They understood, number one, how important that left tackle is for this football program that's based itself on the running game more so than anything else. And there's a history of really good left tackles in the program."

That lineage includes Joe Panos, whom Lucas described as the anchor of the offensive line on the 1993 team that went to the Rose Bowl. Add to the elite list Chris McIntosh, who went on to become athletic director at Wisconsin, as well as his teammate, Aaron Gibson.

But it's Thomas who remains the best offensive tackle Wisconsin has ever produced, according to Lucas.

"It's a position of respect," Lucas said, adding, "I think people understood how good he was. I really do. It was just not a secret. And even for an offensive lineman, he stood out. There were just little plays like a bubble screen where they'd have Joe run down-field and take down the cornerback. I mean, just for the novice in the stands, they could see this cat had some athleticism, but many don't in that position. What Joe was able to do was combine that athleticism with his mental acuity with ability to process the play. When I think of Joe on the field, it's cool, calm, collected. He was always a big proponent of control, balance and stability in the way he played."

Thomas' position coach, Bob Palcic, served up the highest compliment a player can have bestowed on him.

"Joe's an example of the type of football player that you want on your football team," he once told a reporter. "If you looked up in the dictionary 'football player,' Joe Thomas' picture should be there."

The 2006 Wisconsin football team went 12-1, 7-1 in the Big Ten, and finished in the top 10 in the nation.

Former Wisconsin quarterback John Stocco called him "one of the best football players who's played at Wisconsin."

"He was something special," he said. "That's for sure."

14

DRAFTED

Joe Thomas's fate in the NFL was decided with a coin toss two months before the draft.

The Cleveland Browns and Tampa Bay Buccaneers finished the 2006 season with identical 4-12 records and the same strength of schedule, .535.* So on Feb. 23, the contest that would affect the destiny of certain players — including Thomas — wasn't a football game but a coin toss between a pair of general managers, Tampa Bay's Bruce Allen and Cleveland's Phil Savage. It took place at the NFL combine in Indianapolis. Allen called heads. It landed on tails, and the order was set. Oakland already had the top pick, followed by Detroit. Next would be Cleveland, then Tampa Bay and Arizona to round out the top five.

Savage told Tony Grossi of The Plain Dealer years later that had the Browns lost the toss, "it would have changed the course of events."

There was a strong chance, had that coin landed on heads, that Joe Thomas would have worn red, orange and pewter and spent his leisure time fishing in the Gulf of Mexico instead of the Great Lakes.**

And Brady Quinn (with whom Thomas had played in the 2003

---

* How close were the Browns and Buccaneers in 2006? On Christmas Eve, Tampa Bay traveled to Cleveland and beat the Browns, 22-7. Each team had lost five of their final six games. They each lost their final game on New Year's Eve and landed at 4-12. Both had identical composite opponent records — 137-119-0 — which defines strength of schedule. Hence the coin toss.

** The additional irony is that all three quarterbacks on Tampa Bay's roster — Jeff Garcia, Bruce Gradkowski and Luke McCown — all figured into the quarterback carousel with the Browns at some point in their careers.

U.S. Army All-American game) might have gone higher in the draft to Cleveland.

The Browns desperately needed something, someone to make a quick impact. Cleveland had been mired in what Plain Dealer columnist Bud Shaw called a "football depression" since 1999. Since reemerging after three dormant years in the late 1990s, the Browns had just one winning season.

Grossi, then the Browns' beat writer with The Plain Dealer, reported that Savage was considering Texas cornerback Aaron Ross for the Browns' second pick. Ross would wind up going at No. 20 to the New York Giants.

At the NFL combine, Thomas stood to lose more than gain. He already was viewed as a lock within the top three picks. But between his affable personality with the media and on-field performance, he wouldn't fall out of that rarified echelon. Writer Dylan Tomlinson covering the combine wrote that Thomas fielded the onslaught of questions as he went under the annual microscope, saying "he handled the attention about as deftly as a blitzing defensive end. He was poised, confident, friendly and funny."

Under the microscope and before the cameras and stopwatches, Thomas ran a 4.92 40-yard dash. (For comparison: Levi Brown, an offensive lineman out of Penn State who would be drafted fifth overall by Detroit, ran it in 5.4.) Thomas was recorded as weighing 311 pounds, having 33¼ inch arm length and 10⅛ inch hand span.

Thomas had an almost laissez-faire attitude toward the combine.

"Everyone wants to prepare for the combine, but nobody wants to prepare for the season that they have to play," he told the Wisconsin State Journal. "I'm not as much worried about getting a tenth better on this drill or that drill because that's not going to help me next season. I'm pretty observant and I really like to break things down all the time."

Shaw referred to Thomas as having run extremely precise "sewing-machine" steps in a lateral drill.

Physical analyses aren't the only thing teams concentrate on at the combine. There is a psychological side, including the Wonderlic test, which measures cognitive ability and problem solving, and sometimes other, strange evaluations.

"The crazy tests that I remember were the psychology tests," Thomas recalled. "They'd sit you down and you'd have a 300-question psychology exam. Some of the questions are just crazy. Would you rather be a dog or a cat? What does 'Never look a gift horse in the mouth' mean? Stuff like that. I don't know what you pull from that."

The day was a nonstop blur of faces and questions.

"It was frustrating because when you're walking into one meeting with one team, they sit you down and they introduce you to 20 scouts and 15 coaches, and then they say, 'OK, go.' You have to remember everybody's name. And then the next room you walk in and they introduce you to everybody and you're thinking about their name, and then they pull out the white board and they show you a play, and then they say, 'OK, now teach us the play we just taught you.' Then the next room you walk in, and they go, 'Sit down, here's 300 questions of psychological testing.' It really stretches your brain for a person like I am. I'm very good at focus. I can laser-focus on one thing; distractions don't exist. . . . And I think that's part of just my background as a left tackle. I'm used to having all the noise around me, all the craziness, and just focusing on my job and my guy, and I'm good at that. But to go all around and think about eight different things and move my brain in a bunch of different places, I'm just not good at that."

Thomas was shuffled from room to room for tests and questions.

"There were six or seven psychologists in there. They would try to pick your brain and get to the bottom of whatever is in your id and your ego or whatnot. It was like a quiz show for them."

One test in particular stands out in his memory.

"They were trying all these little experiments on you. One of them had this semi-circle suction cup. They'd fold it over, and it would sit up on a table. At a random moment, it would just pop up in the air. They told you, 'Try to catch this as close to the table as possible.' They're testing how quickly your eyes could talk to your brain and your brain could talk to your hand — so you can catch it, right? I did it — I think they gave me two or three times — and the guy said, 'You're the second-best person who's ever done this. The quickest I ever had was Reggie Bush.' I was, 'Oh, I feel pretty good about myself.' Reggie Bush was the number two pick the year before. You know, he was pretty quick. I was feeling pretty good walking out of that one. That was about the only room that I really felt pretty good about."

Speculation continued about Thomas possibly going to Detroit, and for his part the Wisconsin native openly said he did not mind that option, that it was close to home.

Meanwhile, as the draft neared, Wisconsin, like all colleges, was gearing up for the fall season with spring workouts. Offensive line coach Bob Palcic, interviewed about up-and-coming Badgers on the line, kept using Thomas as an athletic barometer. "That was the one position I didn't have to worry about last season, and I didn't care who we were playing against," he told Mike Lucas of The Capital Times. "We're going to miss Joe tremendously."

Palcic, who had swung through a series of coaching jobs, had been part of the Browns' staff in 1999. "I'm a Cleveland Browns guy," he told Marla Ridenour of the Akron Beacon Journal: "I hope it falls right and Cleveland is able to draft him. They won't be sorry. They're getting a terrific player who still has upside. If you take Joe Thomas, you're getting a guy without baggage. I'll stake my life and reputation on it. He's a great leader, a team guy, unselfish, wants to be the best. Everyone who comes here says, 'Bob, are there any holes in him?' I've been looking for them for over a year."

Meanwhile, in Tampa Bay, with his team holding the fourth pick, coach Jon Gruden publicly held hope the Buccaneers could draft Thomas, "The kid, Joe Thomas, from Wisconsin, is a hell of an offensive tackle," he told a Florida Today reporter. "Are you kidding me? . . . This is what we need in Tampa."

The only foregone conclusion of the NFL draft was that the Oakland Raiders would take Louisiana State University quarterback JaMarcus Russell with the No. 1 pick. The Raiders were coming off a 2-14 season. Many fans might still remember the hype around Russell. Probably few, though, can recall the Raiders quarterback on the 2006 team: Andrew Walter.* At least one former player, Tim Brown (an eventual Hall of Famer), urged Oakland to take Thomas with the first pick. "It's not the glamorous move, and it's not the splash everybody wants," he told the Los Angeles Times. "But from a football point of view, it would make perfect sense."

Almost every forecast for Thomas as a pro prospect was glowing — save for one. Ridenour cited Nolan Nawrocki's assessment in Pro Football Weekly's 2007 Draft Preview, which said Thomas was "not very tough" and "shows no killer instinct" and "too often looks content doing just enough to get the job done." He also said Thomas might never be an "elite left tackle" — yet still projected he would be a 10-year starter. Being that an NFL player's average career is 3.3 years, starting for 10 years in the league would be desirable.

Thomas was quoted by Jason Wilde of the Wisconsin State Journal about having a mean streak, saying: "I think it's where it needs to be. I'm not afraid to turn that switch on when I get on that field. If somebody deserves it, they're going to get it."

Thomas visited four teams in one week: Tampa Bay, Detroit, Washington (which had the sixth pick) and Cleveland.

"I don't feel it's necessary and a good use of my time to visit every team," he told the Detroit News.

And then it was time. On April 28, 2007, while Joe Thomas was fishing with friends and family on a lake in Wisconsin, NFL Commissioner Roger Goodell strode to the podium onstage at Radio City Music Hall in New York City to kick off the NFL draft.

That year's draft would be marked by two moments — one inside, and one outside, the football world.

Television networks employ storylines when covering sports. If two potential Hall of Fame pitchers are facing off in a postseason

---

* Walter's first start in his NFL career came on Oct. 1, 2006, against Cleveland. He was 9-for-23 passing for 68 yards with a touchdown to Randy Moss and one interception. The Browns won, 24-21.

game, that's the story. If a college quarterback transfers, and his new team meets his old one — that's the story. If a coach's son goes up against his dad across the sidelines? Story. For the 2007 NFL draft, the storyline quickly became Brady Quinn.

Multiple times during the draft, the TV cameras focused on Quinn, looking like a young investment banker at a reception, wearing a vest without a sports coat, sipping water. Analysts quickly picked up on what was happening: He was falling in the draft. Cameras caught his reaction every time a name other than his own was called. Deion Sanders interviewed him, almost pitying him, about the waiting game. As teams selected players they needed, Quinn, projected to go high, waited.

He kept dropping.

The non-football story occurred 12 days prior to the draft, when the deadliest school shooting took place at a college campus. Thirty-two people — mostly students — were killed at Virginia Tech University. Several people in attendance — including Russell, Goodell and the network analysts — wore Virginia Tech pins.

As expected, Russell, who had skipped his final year of eligibility at LSU, was taken first. On paper, it was a good match. Oakland needed a quarterback, and the 6-6 Russell had played in the Southeastern Conference, arguably the nation's most competitive conference. In January, Russell had led the Tigers to a 41-14 victory over Notre Dame, quarterbacked by Quinn.

With the second pick, Detroit selected Calvin Johnson, the wide receiver from Georgia Tech. He had also declared for the draft a year early.

Then came Cleveland's turn. The cameras zoomed in on Goodell. "With the third pick in the 2007 NFL draft," the commissioner announced, "the Cleveland Browns select left tackle Joe Thomas, Wisconsin." Without Thomas to focus on, because he had opted for the fishing trip back home, the cameras instead picked out a rabid Browns fan in the crowd. The next shot was of Quinn, sipping water. It would be a long night for the Notre Dame quarterback.

Thomas was the first offensive tackle the Browns took in the first round since Bob McKay in 1970.*

He was also the highest pick ever from Wisconsin. (Offensive lineman Paul Gruber had gone No. 4 overall in 1988 to Tampa Bay.) Somewhat surprisingly, he was the sole player drafted from Wisconsin in 2007.

Reportedly, there had been a split in the front office over the No. 3 spot. Browns general manager Phil Savage wanted Thomas; offensive coordinator Rob Chudzinski wanted Quinn. Savage had telegraphed his intent weeks earlier, when speaking at a Browns Backers event. He told that crowd about being with Baltimore a decade earlier when the Ravens chose offensive lineman Jonathan Ogden with the fourth pick in 1996. The Plain Dealer's Mary Kay Cabot recalled Savage's comments in a story, saying he remembered the choice of Ogden was not an "exciting" pick, but it bore fruit. Ogden became a Hall of Famer. "Picking Joe Thomas may not be the most exciting pick, but it could be the wisest thing for us to do at this point. We'll see how it all plays out."**

In the days leading up to the draft, Thomas had been optimistic about Cleveland. Cabot quoted him as saying he would be "ecstatic" if the Browns selected him at No. 3. "It's a great organization and great city, and I think I'd be a good fit in Cleveland," he said. "My dad's side of the family is from Toledo and we'd go out to Findlay for family reunions."

As Thomas continued fishing in Wisconsin, the draft continued in New York.

When Atlanta was up at No. 8, ESPN split the screen between Goodell and Quinn. Moments later, draft guru Mike Mayock said Quinn should go at No. 9 to Miami. But the Dolphins took Ted Ginn

---

* McKay turned out to be a solid pick out of Texas, 21st overall. He played the first six of his nine seasons with the Browns. Like Thomas, he enjoyed hunting and fishing. Also, the 1970 and 2007 drafts had some comparable traits. It was a quarterback who went first in both. In 1970, Pittsburgh drafted Terry Bradshaw. And the Browns had the No. 3 pick and chose a quarterback — Mike Phipps out of Purdue.

** In 2013, Ogden was a first-ballot Hall of Fame selection.

Jr. of Ohio State. When Houston came up at No. 10, the Texans chose Amobi Okoye, a defensive tackle out of Louisville. As San Francisco neared its No. 11 pick, the split screen was gone. Broadcaster Rich Eisen told the crowd Goodell had invited Quinn to his green room, where there were no cameras.

When Pittsburgh was up with the No. 15 pick, the network's Adam Schefter forecast what would happen with Quinn: "We also turn our attention to Brady Quinn. And I think what you're going to see happen is there were so many teams who were planning to take a quarterback at the top of round two. One of them now, at an unexpected time, is probably going to try to trade up to get a guy like Brady Quinn. You're talking about maybe the Cleveland Browns, maybe the Miami Dolphins, maybe the Minnesota Vikings. But somebody is going to come up unexpectedly, see the value in Brady Quinn, and pull an unexpected deal and take him. But at this point in time Brady has lost $20 million and counting."

Then came the No. 22 pick, slated to go to Dallas. But an announcement was made: Cleveland had traded its second-round selection and 2008 first-round pick to Dallas to move up to No. 22 in the first round. After four hours of waiting, sipping water and hanging out in the commissioner's green room, Brady Quinn — who as a kid had a Browns poster hanging in his bedroom — was going to Cleveland. He would be reunited with Thomas, with whom he had played back in 2003 at the U.S. Army game in San Antonio.

Schefter was effusive about the Browns' first two picks, "Cleveland has come away with Joe Thomas and Brady Quinn, hail Phil Savage!"

In a Plain Dealer story a week after the draft, Savage called this "the day the fortunes of the Browns turned around."

"It couldn't have worked out any better," Quinn told Grossi. "I have the opportunity to play with a great left tackle and, hopefully, we'll be playing a long time together."

The rest of Cleveland's 2007 picks and their round taken: Cornerback Eric Wright (second), cornerback Brandon McDonald (fifth), defensive end Melila Purcell (sixth), defensive end Chase Pittman (seventh) and receiver Syndric Steptoe (seventh).

But all eyes were focused on Thomas, the Browns' big catch. On July 26, 2007, Thomas and the team agreed to a contract totaling $42.5 million, with about $23 million guaranteed.*

The Plain Dealer's Bud Shaw called the draft "better safe than sexy" for a team with an abysmal rushing game. File this under Thank God for Detroit: The Browns finished the 2006 season ranked 31st in rushing yards.

"Joe Thomas was the right thing to do," Savage told Shaw during the draft.

One downside of the draft for Thomas: It ended his track and field career. He had been hoping to compete in the Big Ten championships taking place at Penn State about two weeks after the draft. Thomas felt confident he could have done well. His agent ran the idea by the Browns, who said no. They didn't want to risk an injury before their top draft pick had even played a down in the NFL. In the end, Thomas did not have regrets, though he admitted it would have been nice for one more competition.

Thomas had spent the last eight years playing on perpetually winning teams — first at Brookfield Central, then at Wisconsin. His eye remained on getting better. While fans are mesmerized by the glamour of quarterbacks and star players, or the scoring potential of those on their fantasy teams, it's the meat and potatoes that counts. Thomas spent his time as a devotee of Seattle Seahawks left tackle Walter Jones, who had been named to the Pro Bowl seven times.

Jones was a good player to emulate at his position. A first-round selection out of Florida State, Jones played in 180 NFL games — all with Seattle. His career was in its twilight as Thomas' was beginning. Jones' last game came in 2008. Thomas predicted he would earn induction to the Hall of Fame. Jones made it in 2014.

Incidentally, in 2014, a fun trivial connection links Wisconsin, the Browns and mirrors the 2007 draft in that Cleveland would be able to land two top players. On April 11, 2014, the movie "Draft

---

* Quinn signed Aug. 7, 2007. He had been working out in Arizona but missed 16 practices.

Day" was released. In it, Kevin Costner stars as Browns general manager Sonny Weaver Jr. One of the players Weaver is considering drafting is Wisconsin quarterback Bo Callahan, played by Josh Pence. In the movie, a clip is shown of Callahan during a Wisconsin game. The footage is of an actual game against Ohio State on Nov. 3, 2007, and the real Wisconsin quarterback shown is Tyler Donovan, completing a long pass (in reality, it was a broken play that ended well for the Badgers). At the time, Thomas was already with the Browns, but he had spent several seasons on the same Wisconsin team with Donovan. And for the record, Thomas attended the premiere at a theater in the Cleveland suburb of Valley View.

The movie ends with Sonny getting his picks, just like Savage was able to do in 2007.

After the draft, Thomas made it clear in interviews he was well aware of the fan base in Cleveland. "If we start winning some games, they're going to anoint us, you know what I mean? That's kind of a cool feeling, being able to hopefully be part of bringing an organization back to glory." Then, on June 18, on a beautiful, 89-degree night at Jacobs Field, Thomas — wearing a No. 73 Browns jersey — threw out the first pitch before a Phillies-Indians game.* Thomas saw a 10-1 rout with Cleveland's Cliff Lee getting the victory. Cole Hamels took the loss. The Indians were on their way to winning the American League Central title. Just as Cleveland baseball fans had felt with their team, Thomas had high hopes going into his rookie season.

Three years later, when the 2010 NFL draft rolled around, neither Quinn nor Savage would be with the team. Wright lasted in the league until 2013, McDonald played to 2012. Steptoe was done in a year, and Purcell and Pittman had fleeting careers with time spent on practice squads. By that point, Thomas had made the Pro Bowl three times. His career was moving ahead, but the hopeful glory days Thomas alluded to would not materialize.

---

* Between training camp, having an offseason home in Madison and other commitments, the Thomases would go to about 10 to 15 games at Progressive Field, previously known as Jacobs Field, during his time in Cleveland.

PART THREE

THE BROWNS
(IN JOE'S WORDS)

15

ROOKIE SEASON

"I guess I should have known that it was a sign of things to come"

After the NFL draft, you don't have a lot of personal time and you get into the thick of things pretty quickly. They rush you to your new city, and you start right away. I was drafted by the Browns on April 28, 2007. The next day I was flown to Cleveland for my introductory press conference. My first rookie minicamp practice was May 4. It's quite the whirlwind considering I had no idea what city I would be living in just a few days before.

I used to get asked a lot about why I switched from my college number 72 to my NFL number 73. It's a pretty simple story. My agent called and told me that somebody already had number 72. It was veteran Ryan Tucker, and he said I could have it for $10,000. I could think of 10,000 things I'd rather spend that on besides a number. I told him that I didn't care at all what my jersey number was. I didn't want to talk about it. I said, "Whatever number the Browns give me is fine."

There was, however, one major thing to do before training camp started in July — sign my first NFL contract. Rookies were allowed to participate in all of the offseason practices without a contract, but once training camp started you had to be under contract.

I told my agent the deal needed to be done because I didn't want to miss any practice time. This was back before the rookie wage scale practically ended holdouts. Back then most first-round picks missed at least some of training camp; it was very common.

I thought, particularly as an offensive lineman, you want to get in there and learn the system. You want to get to know the coaches and the guys you are going to play next to. My first goal was to start from day one and I knew the best way to get that done was to get to camp on time and get the deal done.

With training camp set to open July 27, the deadline was approaching. I had seen stories about the Browns' first-round offensive picks before me who missed a lot of training camp. Tight end Kellen Winslow Jr. in 2004 and wide receiver Braylon Edwards in 2005 missed the first 12 and 13 days of training camp, respectively. I was never one to pry into someone's personal business, but I knew I didn't want that to be me.

On the eve of the start of training camp, I was in my back yard with my wife. I was trying to steal internet from my neighbors when my offensive line coach Steve Marshall called. He put on the full-court press — "We need you in camp, I understand it's a business, but tell your agent to get this deal done" — that kind of thing. He was trying to apply some hard pressure, and that's when I realized we aren't in Kansas anymore. This is truly a business. My agent went to work, and later that day, July 26, we agreed to terms on a six-year contract. I was officially a Cleveland Brown and I was stoked to be able to fully participate in all practices.

Back then two-a-day practices were the norm, which made training camp a bit of a grind. You would have two practices one day, then you had one practice the next, then you had two again, so you kind of alternated. That year our two-a-day practices were at 8:45-10:45 a.m. and 5:30-7:30 p.m. In a seven-day week you would get about 10-12 practices in. You were getting a lot of time on the field and a lot of hitting, a lot of opportunity to get yourself up to speed. Everything was new — new drills, new techniques, new teammates — so I was glad I got my deal signed and was able to jump right in as opposed to missing some time and potentially falling behind. I was fortunate to get my deal done and be in on time.

Brady Quinn, however, didn't get his deal done until about two weeks into camp, solidifying Charlie Frye as our starting quarterback.

I didn't know what to expect from my teammates. I remember walking into the locker room, going around introducing myself and shaking everyone's hand. I approached Ted Washington. He was a defensive tackle in his 17th season in the league and here I was as a 22-year-old rookie, who had been on the planet for just five years more than he had been in the NFL. He was generously listed at 375 pounds. I walked up to him and tried to introduce myself. I stretched my hand out, and he promptly told me that rookies can't touch him and he walked away.*

Luckily, I got to work alongside other friendlier teammates like veteran left guard Eric Steinbach. The Browns signed him during free agency that season in March. He entered the NFL as a second-round pick by the Cincinnati Bengals in 2003 and started 62 games during four years with the Bengals. He was considered one of the top left guards in the league. I was excited to pick his brain, especially about his familiarity with the AFC North.

Having a guy who had a lot of knowledge about the division playing next to me was really helpful, especially early on because we opened up at home that year against Pittsburgh, and then we played the Bengals in Week 2. It allowed me to use his experience to help me understand not only the scheme but the individual players and what the challenges of playing against other NFL players are.

Steinbach was a great mentor and showed me how to be a pro on the field, but he preferred to take an all-natural approach to film study — basically, not much at all. He just wanted to react in the game instead of thinking too much about the opponent. I turned out to be the total opposite. But he really helped show me what it took to be a pro, and I think he is one of the best players in NFL history to never make a Pro Bowl. He had many deserving seasons, including the one we were about to embark upon.

The season opener was at home and I was pumped. FirstEnergy Stadium is one of the best stadiums in the league. It's right on the

---

* Washington played the final two of his 17 years in Cleveland, retiring after Thomas' rookie season. His father was a linebacker for Houston from 1973 to 1982.

water and on the edge of downtown. They have real grass, which I always loved playing on. But the fans are what make the stadium so unique. These are passionate, loyal fans. The team has such a rich tradition. The Dawg Pound brings an attitude that we can feel on the field. We played some preseason games, but there is just nothing like going through the tunnel during a real NFL game for the first time.

There were nerves. Not quite as bad as my first college game, but it was nerve-racking. There's also a lot of pressure because you are the first-round pick. You want to try to prove those people right who believed in you. This is your job now. It's not just for fun like it was in college. This is your profession. There's a new level of pressure. It's a man's game.

We were playing the Pittsburgh Steelers and what was about to happen was truly a welcome to the NFL moment for me. We lost 34-7, but it was what happened around halftime and in the next couple days that was a real eye-opener. We played a bad first half. No doubt about it. It was 17-0 and the coaching staff decided it was time to pull Charlie Frye. Benching him wasn't enough, though; two days later he was traded to Seattle.

It was my rookie season, and for all I knew, Charlie Frye was the next Peyton Manning. He was from Willard, Ohio, and played his college ball at Akron in Ohio. In my mind he was going to be the homegrown hero that was going to take us to the Super Bowl. In the first half, he took five sacks, tossed an interception and only threw for 34 yards. As a rookie, I'm thinking, "OK, second half, we are going to come back and win this thing." Then we find out that Charlie had been benched and that Derek Anderson would be the starter. Derek came in and played pretty well, but we got our butts whipped.

Then Charlie was traded for a sixth-round pick. The guy we spent the whole offseason with. He did things to bring the team together. He organized a team-bonding outing on Lake Erie. He was going to be our fearless leader and take us to the Super Bowl. Instead he got traded after the first game of my NFL career.

In a span of 48 hours, Charlie was uprooted and went from Cleveland's starting quarterback to Seattle's third-string quarterback.

That's how fast things can change in the National Football League. We made NFL history. We were the first team to trade their Week 1 starter before Week 2. I guess I should have known that it was a sign of things to come. It showed me there were no loyalties, no feelings — it's a cold-blooded business. Teams will make rash decisions if it will help them win games and save their jobs. I learned the NFL was a business real fast.

I also learned real fast what going against an elite NFL pass rusher was like. That first game I was up against James Harrison. Yes, the guy who would go on to be the 2008 NFL Defensive Player of the Year, finish his career with 84.5 sacks and make five Pro Bowls. I'll be honest: Heading into that game I had no idea who James Harrison was. Our coaching staff knew though, and our head coach Romeo Crennel was worried about the matchup because he would ask me in team meetings if I was ready for Harrison's speed and power moves.

We ended that Steelers game giving up six total sacks. Throughout the game I felt like Harrison had all six of them. He was so strong, so powerful and was like no one else I faced in college. Everything went terribly, and I just felt like I wasn't doing my job because things were going so badly. It wasn't until that next day — the day Charlie got traded — when we sat down and reviewed the film with our coaches and there was plenty for me to improve on, but they kind of gave me an "Atta boy. That's a nice start for a rookie." Officially Harrison only had half of a sack. I had thought I got my ass kicked. I couldn't believe they thought that I played decently.

That helped give me a little more confidence heading into Week 2. We were playing the Bengals and my matchup wasn't any easier. I went against another top edge rusher in Justin Smith, who finished his career with five Pro Bowls and 87 career sacks. He was a big, strong guy but had different attributes than Harrison. I knew that I had to jump set him all game or else I would get run over because he was so big and so strong.* The only problem with that was I

---

* A jump set is a specific way for offensive linemen to defend on pass-protection plays. It involves knowing the defender's moves, taking a specific angle and gaining leverage.

would get beat immediately if I tried to jump set him and he chose an inside rush.

I really hit the film room hard. I needed to find a tell that would let me know pre-snap when he was rushing inside. I watched his tendencies, his hand placement. I studied, and I studied hard. I watched and charted his stance and rush snap after snap after snap. After watching enough film, I realized he would change his stance and put his inside foot and hand back in his stance when he was going inside. I knew that if I saw this I could set back and react to the inside move, but outside of that I would jump set the rest. So I put together a different game plan for facing him than I had for Harrison. After that first game, I wasn't sure what to expect, but I knew all I could do was focus on my job and work to improve.

That second game ended up being one of the most memorable of my career, maybe even the most fun. Statistically, it was the best offensive output I was a part of for a single game in my career. We scored 51 points. The rest of my career we never scored more than 41 in a game. We put up 554 scrimmage yards. We never reached more than 430 in any of my other games.

It was like the opposite feeling of our opener against the Steelers. We just felt like we were going to score a touchdown every time we had the ball, and we basically did. We won 51-45. Our running back Jamal Lewis rushed for 216 yards. Derek Anderson threw for 328 yards with five touchdowns. We didn't give up a sack the entire game and I held my own with Justin Smith because his tell proved to be almost 100 percent accurate. That was when I thought, "I can do this. Now I have to prove each week that I can do it. I need to keep working, but I belong here." I also knew that film study and having an individual game plan for each pass rusher was my key to sustained success in the NFL. This wasn't college anymore. Everyone is really good. I learned if I put in the work I could out game-plan my opponents. I needed to have a different plan for everyone I faced to help take advantage of their weaknesses. I had to put in the work to get my job done and that was exactly what I planned to do to help put my team in the best position to win each week.

We faced a gauntlet of top tier pass rushers my rookie season. In addition to Harrison and Smith, I also went up against Mario Williams and Jason Taylor.

Williams was the No. 1 overall pick in 2006. He finished his career with 97.5 sacks and four Pro Bowls. Taylor was selected to the Pro Football Hall of Fame in 2017. He registered 139.5 career sacks, made six Pro Bowls, was the NFL sack leader in 2002 and was the reigning NFL Defensive Player of the Year.

Taylor had such long arms and used them to beat tackles for 15 seasons. He always would stick his long arm into a tackle's chest and then reach around and grab the back of your shoulder pad when you'd try to grab his chest, and at that point you were beat. After watching a ton of film, I reasoned that the best way to beat him was to just keep his long arms away from me. But how would I do that? How could I do that? I decided to take a chance and do something unorthodox. Instead of trying to grab his chest, which I knew wasn't going to work because his arms were too long, I was going to try to punch his hand like he was holding a boxing training mitt. This, in theory, would keep him away from me so he couldn't grab my pads. I practiced it all week against the scout team. When their hand went out, I reached out and just punched it. I felt ready for game day.

When I employed it during the game Jason didn't know what to make of it. It worked perfectly, and he was dumbfounded until the fourth quarter when he finally just kind of gave up and tried to do his other less effective pass-rush moves. They were less effective because he never really needed to work on them because he never really needed them. This was another situation where putting in the time in the film room gave me an advantage over my opponent.

We ended up winning both of those games against the Texans and Dolphins, which was always the most important thing. After getting crushed in the opener, we rolled off wins in seven of our next 10 games. But we took things one game at a time. We headed into the second-to-last game of the season at Cincinnati with a 9-5 record and needing a win to control our own destiny in the playoffs. The Bengals were 5-9, and we had put on a show offensively in that

Week 2 matchup. It's the NFL though, and you never take an opponent lightly.

The game was really bad weather. Winds were gusting around 30 mph. But no excuses, we had a clunker. We lost 19-14. I still think we were the better team. We just didn't play well. Sometimes you just have clunkers. That's just the way it is. But that game put us behind the eight ball for the playoffs. We won the season finale to finish with a 10-6 record. The Steelers also finished 10-6 and had the tiebreaker so they won the AFC North Division. Our playoff hopes came down to the Colts-Titans game on Sunday Night Football.

The Colts were 13-2 and had nothing to play for. They had already clinched their division and the No. 2 seed in the playoffs. The Titans were 9-6 and would clinch a Wild Card playoff spot with a win. If the Titans lost, the Wild Card spot would go to us.

The Colts had Peyton Manning, one of the best to play the quarterback position. He also had never missed a start in his career, a streak that was at 159 games at that point. We knew he would at least start, but we didn't know exactly how long he would play. It was a weird feeling watching in my basement knowing there was nothing I could do but watch, fearing the Colts would pull Manning and starters right away to avoid potential injuries and essentially lose on purpose. During pregame, the cameras panned to a Titans player who looked into the lens and said something to the extent of, "Have fun watching the playoffs from home Cleveland."

Manning did start and extended his streak, but he didn't play long. The Colts benched him in the second quarter and brought in my former college teammate, Jim Sorgi. I am an eternal optimist, perhaps even to a flaw. I knew Sorgi was no Manning, but I watched with hope. At the end, there was 2:56 left in the fourth quarter and the Colts were down, 16-10, with the ball. How many times have we seen Manning put together a two-minute game-winning drive? Alas, it wasn't Manning, it was Sorgi who threw three incomplete passes to end the game. My eternal hope ran dry. Our playoff hopes went down in flames as the Titans claimed that last playoff spot.

At the end of the year, they announced I made the Pro Bowl. I thought, "Wow, I really snuck into that one" because I felt I played OK but had room for improvement. It was always an honor to represent the Browns and Browns fans at the Pro Bowl, but I would have traded it for a shot at the playoffs.

It was a roller coaster of a season. I felt good about the talent on the team and our prospects going forward. It's tough to look back now and know that would end up being my only winning season in Cleveland.

16

ALL THOSE QUARTERBACKS

"Boy, was I wrong about what the worst-case scenario was."

One of the things I get asked the most about from my career was the quarterbacks. How many were there? Who was the best? Who was the worst? Can I name them all? Most days I can name them all, but it takes a little bit of thinking. It's also hard because does that question mean just the starting quarterbacks?

A total of 20 different players started at quarterback during my tenure with the Browns. For you math geeks, I played 11 seasons so that's almost two a year. I played 167 games so that's an average of a new quarterback every 8.35 games. Derek Anderson started the most with 34, while five (Charlie Frye, Bruce Gradkowski, Thad Lewis, Connor Shaw and Kevin Hogan) started just one. Only three started 20 or more games (Anderson, Colt McCoy and Brandon Weeden). Most years we were down to our third-string quarterback before the season ended. I would have loved the opportunity to play with one guy an entire season, year after year, but that's just not how it went for a variety of reasons.

There were also a few (Charlie Whitehurst and Josh Johnson) that came in as a backup and played but didn't ever technically start a game. And there are Josh Cribbs and Terrelle Pryor, who came in as wide receivers and played a lot of quarterback. Do they count, too? I say yes. Let's cover them all starting with the first quarterback for my very first start: Charlie Frye.

I've talked about Charlie before. He was a part of my welcome-to-the-NFL moment. He was our starting quarterback heading into my rookie season. A local kid. He was benched by halftime of the season opener and traded days after. That last sentence still amazes me. He was our starter the entire offseason and was benched and traded within hours. It just goes to show you how quick things can change in the NFL.

Derek Anderson came in for Charlie and started the rest of the 2007 season. He went 10-5 as a starter my rookie year. He made the Pro Bowl. He was the only quarterback who made a Pro Bowl while I was playing with them. DA could really sling it. He had such a strong arm. Off the field, he was a funny guy. A real goof. He never took himself too seriously. He was just a fun guy to be around.

I remember that Pro Bowl we went to together. The quarterbacks for the AFC were DA along with Peyton Manning and Ben Roeth-lisberger. The first day we were all out laying by the pool. It was in Hawaii, so we were enjoying it. Now, DA was from Scappoose, Oregon. They must not get too much sun there because he decided he didn't want to wear any sunscreen. After that first day he was burnt to a crisp, bright red all over. So all the quarterbacks called him Lobster Boy the rest of the trip. He even had a hard time putting his pads on for the game because it hurt so bad. Let's just say he didn't play the best game in Pro Bowl history and, of course, he blamed it on the sunburn.

The next quarterback was Brady Quinn. We were very close. The same draft class, both first-round picks. We were roommates that first year. Brady was from Ohio, but you would have thought he was from California. He was that prototypical California beach guy who looked like he belonged in a boy band. He took his physique very seriously and never missed a workout even when we went on vacations together.

Our rookie year we had to endure typical rookie hazing. The vets would do anything to try to embarrass you in front of the group. One thing I had to do during training camp was every time I entered the cafeteria, I had to wear a giant pointy fairy godmother-type hat. I didn't mind. It was all in good fun. Once camp came to a close, the vets decided that all the rookies had to shave their heads. For me, I was only worried about my hair not growing back. I knew I was on borrowed time and obviously that has since caught up to me. We all got our heads shaved. My hair did eventually grow back. However, Brady had a Subway commercial set to film shortly after, and they ended up having to delay the filming of it. If you go back and watch it, you can see that his hair was still pretty short and closely resembled his recent buzz cut. It wasn't his normal flowing California dreamboat hair in the commercial.

Ken Dorsey was the next to get a start under center — or should I say Coach Ken. He's having a great career now as a coach, and you could see it back then. He was super smart. He knew the entire offense frontward and backward. He knew where everyone should be at all times. He was a huge help for the other quarterbacks with game planning and with preparation. You knew his future was in coaching. He didn't have the arm strength like Derek Anderson did. He wasn't able to stretch the defense, but he had the brains to operate the offense. He was a great leader.

After injuries to DA, Brady and Ken in 2008, we had no quarterbacks left. We signed Bruce Gradkowski late in the season, and he started the season finale for us. Bruce was from Pittsburgh, and that last game was in Pittsburgh. Before that game, he had the o-line over to his house for an epic meal. His mom, aunts and cousins served us so much food—a traditional Italian meal. It was so neat to be a part of that because you could tell this was something his family did often, and it was really cool. Even though most of the family members at that party were wearing Steelers gear, it was great to see how tight knit they were. The spread was enormous. Everyone in his family brought a plate and there was lasagna and every type of pasta dish you could imagine. His start the next day was one to forget — five completions for 18 yards, two picks and three sacks in a 31-0 loss — but Bruce went on to have a solid career as a backup quarterback. He was the kind of guy teams wanted to keep around because he was such a good locker-room guy.

In 2010, Mike Holmgren revamped the quarterback room and brought in three new guys. The initial starter was Jake Delhomme and we all were excited. There was a different feel about what he brought to the team. He was probably the most heralded quarterback I played with. He made a Pro Bowl and took Carolina to the Super Bowl. Now, all those accomplishments came before he joined Cleveland, but when he got in the huddle I remember thinking, "Wow. This is what it is supposed to look like." Watching him go through the progressions was a thing of beauty. He would get rid of the ball so quickly and to exactly where it was supposed to go. He made lightning-quick decisions. He was one of the most liked teammates, and everyone believed in him. It was unfortunate that injuries limited him to only four starts with the Browns. He put together a 2-2 record, but that was the second-best winning percentage any of my starting quarterbacks had.

Jake had an easy-going southern personality. He was charismatic, always positive and gregarious. Jake was from Louisiana, played his college ball at Southwestern Louisiana. Prior to Cleveland, he spent his time in the NFL with New Orleans and Carolina. Needless to say, he didn't have a lot of experience with Midwestern winters. I took him ice fishing, and he was just amazed that it got so cold up here that you could actually walk on the water. He spent more time drilling holes, like my kids do when I take them, than he did fishing. When it was time to head home our pond looked like Swiss cheese, but that was Jake, just a happy-positive guy who was always curious to learn.

After Jake got hurt Seneca Wallace came in. Seneca was the first quarterback who I played with who was just a pure athlete. If you missed your block, more likely than not he would be able to get on the move and avoid taking the sack. He was so good at throwing on the run. That ability to escape was so rare. The first guy to him hardly ever took him down. The fact that he could just throw bullets while on the run was impressive. Injuries really plagued him as well as he was limited to just four starts that season.

After Seneca went down it led us to our third-string quarterback that season, a rookie who we selected in the third round that year, Colt McCoy. The plan was for Colt, whose real name is Daniel, to come in and learn under savvy vets in Jake and Seneca, but he was thrown to the fire right away due to injuries.

Colt came in and had tremendous confidence. He was accurate and could really see a defense. The night before his first game, the coach had him stand up in front of the team and address us. He captivated the room. He oozed charisma. He told a story about how he and his brother got permission to deer hunt on a ranch in Texas and they accidentally shot the owner's prize steer. Now, what that had to do with football or what the punch line was, I don't remember, but what I do remember was he just had this swagger that he made you believe that was he going to win this game and every game. He had true leadership qualities, and people were drawn to him.

After a solid performance in a loss to the Steelers in his first start, he led us to upset victories against the defending Super Bowl champion New Orleans Saints in the Superdome and then to a win at home against the New England Patriots. Those were two of my favorite victories. In New Orleans, our punter Reggie Hodges had the longest run of the game, a 68-yard run on a fake punt. It was great to go down there and beat them decidedly, 30-17.

We rarely had two wins back-to-back in my career, let alone two butt-kicking wins, but that's just what happened as we took down the Patriots, 34-14, the next week. That one stands out because it was the only time I beat Bill Belichick or Tom Brady in a game. Our head coach Pat Shurmur was fired after the 2012 season and Colt was traded to San Francisco, but he went on to have a long successful career as a backup quarterback.

First-round pick Brandon Weeden was the next one under center. I'm sure everyone remembers that he was a 28-year-old rookie. He had spent several years in the minor-league system of Major League Baseball as a pitcher. He was the first player selected by the Yankees in 2002. I was always fascinated listening to his stories about playing minor-league ball — busing all over the country and not staying in the best accommodations. Brandon had an amazing arm. He could fit the ball into the tightest windows and had the most amazing zip I have seen. It was like a rocket coming out of his hands.

Thad Lewis was next. What I remember about him was that he was really popular in the locker room. A friendly guy, always laughing, fun to be around. He's another one of the guys who had just one start with us and it was of course a season finale at Pittsburgh. And like almost all of the others, it didn't go very well. We lost 24-10 in the last game of the 2012 season.

Brian Hoyer the Destroyer came in 2013. He was from Cleveland and played high school ball at St. Ignatius. He was with New England for four seasons prior to joining the Browns. He saw firsthand in Tom Brady the things that a great quarterback does. He brought those things to the team. He knew how important team chemistry was and how vital it was to build strong bonds with your teammates, especially your linemen. He did a great job with that. He really helped bring the team together.

Brian, whose real name is Axel, came in and played really well. He helped us win all three of his starts in 2013 before a knee injury sidelined him for the rest of the season. Then in 2014, he led us to a great start. We were 7-4. Our coaches, especially our offensive coordinator Kyle Shanahan, really liked and believed in him. He struggled in a couple of our next games, and it was unfortunate because we had a first-round pick waiting on the bench and the call was made to replace Hoyer. A lot of us felt he had earned that spot and he kind of got a raw deal. Hoyer was the only quarterback who finished with a winning percentage above .500 with me, as he went 10-6 as a starter (.625).

That first-round pick who came in was Johnny Manziel. Johnny was very misunderstood. I really liked him as a person. I think everyone liked him. He just didn't understand the commitment level it took to be a starting quarterback in the NFL. He wasn't willing to do that. But because of his draft status he was given the keys to the franchise when he just wasn't ready. We players knew it. We saw it in practice.

To be an NFL quarterback, you have to be committed to the

game. That commitment will take you away from friends and family. It's a huge commitment, and only a few are willing to make it. If you don't, you almost certainly won't have success in the NFL. I talked with Johnny about it, but if you aren't a quarterback, it's hard to tell a quarterback what to do. Plus no one can talk you into doing it, you have to be self-motivated.

A few years after playing with Johnny, he was a guest on my podcast with former teammate Andrew Hawkins. He came on and he apologized to me. He said he felt like he not only squandered his own career, but that he wasted years of my career. He didn't have to say that, but I really respected him for that. His biggest downside was that he couldn't say no. That is something you need to learn to do as a professional athlete. Friends, family and lots of people come to you for things all the time and you need to be able to say no. Johnny just couldn't do that. He had too many friends taking him away from what he needed to do to be a successful NFL quarterback.

Toughness is also something an NFL quarterback needs, and Connor Shaw was one of the toughest I played with. He had just one start, the 2014 season finale. We were playing at Baltimore with nothing on the line for us, despite one of our better records that year. We were 7-8 but mathematically eliminated from the playoffs. Baltimore was 9-6 and fighting for a playoff spot. Connor was a competitor. He was willing to die out there to give us a chance to win. He had so much desire. He helped us take a 7-3 lead into the fourth quarter, but Baltimore scored 17 fourth-quarter points to seal a 20-10 win.

Another thing to know about Connor is that he was born in Georgia and went to school at South Carolina, and he had a thick southern accent. It was so thick it was hard to understand him in the huddle. We knew early in the week that he was going to start that last game. We were on the practice field in the huddle, and he called a play for probably the first time with the first-string offense. I had to stop him and say, 'Hey man, I'm really sorry, but no one can understand what the fuck you are saying. You are going to have to either say it twice or slow it down.' He ended up repeating the play twice most of that week and during the game.

We went from Connor, who was bald, to Josh McCown, who probably had the best head of hair of all my teammates. I'd always watch with jealousy as he would comb it to perfection in front of a mirror after a Friday practice before he went home to his kids who were older than me. You wouldn't know it by looking at him and his great hair, but Josh was an athletic freak. He came in one day and showed us the cutups of him playing wide receiver for the Lions in 2006. Until then, I don't think anyone on our team realized what a great athlete he was. The Lions had him play slot receiver for a few games at the end of the season and he looked good. The other thing is, he is a sick basketball player. I've seen videos of him dunking, and his leaping ability is off the charts.

Josh was also one of the best leaders I ever played with. He had this ability to just grab the huddle, command respect, make everyone listen and believe in him. This is not a knock on Josh, but he was also probably the hardest quarterback that I had to block for. He couldn't stand to just throw the ball away. He was such a competitor. If the first, second, third, fourth targets were not open, he would keep looking. He would just hang in there as long as he possibly could before he would get absolutely creamed. I think that's how he got his collarbone broken with us. He made a lot of great plays late in the shot clock. He made a lot of great throws, but he also took a lot of massive hits because he was such a competitor. For reasons like that, everyone loved him on that team. It didn't matter what position you played or what walk of life you came from, he was loved by everyone.

Nothing really stands out about Austin Davis from his two starts with the Browns, and I don't know if that's good or bad, but I do know that one game he played in was extremely memorable. It was 2015 and we were hosting the Ravens on Monday Night Football. Josh McCown started the game, but an injury forced him out in the fourth quarter. We were down, 27-20, when Austin came in. Late in the game he engineered a great drive, completing all six of his passes and taking us 71 yards culminating in a 42-yard touchdown pass to Travis Benjamin. The score was tied, 27-27, with 1:47 remaining. On defense, Tramon Williams intercepted a pass giving us the ball at the Ravens' 46-yard line with 50 seconds remaining. Austin completed a short 6-yard pass to Brian Hartline, then scrambled for 7 yards on the next play. We were down to the Ravens' 33-yard line with three ticks left on the clock. We came out and attempted a 51-yard field goal. It's a long field goal and I remember thinking, "Let's hit this for the win and worst-case scenario, we miss and we head to overtime." Boy, was I wrong about what the worst-case scenario was. Our field-goal attempt was blocked and returned 64 yards for a Ravens touchdown. Game over. We lose.

Robert Griffin III, or RGIII, was the last quarterback to start a game for me that I won. That also happened two years before I retired. I loved RGIII. He was super confident. He wasn't afraid to be himself. He wasn't afraid to talk about himself. I remember that he used to always bring his boombox into the shower and I remember thinking to myself: "We live such different lives that he needs a soundtrack everywhere he goes. Even when in the shower he needs to be a DJ." On the field, he was another guy who showed flashes of brilliance, but injuries limited him to just five games. You could see why he was a track star, why he won the Heisman Trophy, why he took the NFL by storm as a rookie. He had all the qualities you look for in a quarterback, but he just didn't stay healthy his one season with the Browns.

There are players who are drafted high that you expect big things out of right away. RGIII is a good example for Washington. He was the No. 2 overall pick so odds were pretty good that he would be on the field very soon. On the other end of the spectrum, sometimes you have a guy you draft a little bit later with the plan of having him kind of taking a backseat for a while and learn the NFL. That was the plan for Cody Kessler.

He wasn't expected to come in and start right away but with some time to develop, you hope he grows into a starter or solid backup. He came in and was firmly behind Josh McCown and RGIII as a rookie. The plan was not for him to start right away, but there we were Week 3 and McCown and Griffin are both out and Cody has to make his NFL debut. He didn't get that time to grow and develop. He was thrown right into the fire. He was an accurate quarterback, but struggled to push the ball down the field with consistency. Cody does, however, have the distinction of being the quarterback who took the final snap on my last NFL play.

DeShone Kizer was a second-round pick in my last NFL season. He was a big, strong guy. He was an Ohio kid. He had passion for the game. He had the physical skills, but it's tough when a rookie is at the helm, because you never know what you are going to get. You don't know how a guy is going to react when you're on the big stage and the lights are bright.

He would do things at times that left you scratching your head. It wasn't just him, it was all rookies, but I remember one game, we had an option play in for our goal-line package. It's a pretty simple play. The quarterback runs to his left and if the defensive end crashes down and takes him, all he has to do is pitch the ball with his left hand to the running back. We practiced it at least 10 times that week. We get to the game and the perfect time comes for that play call. We line up, DeShone takes the snap and starts moving down the line of scrimmage. The defensive end crashed down right at him, but instead of flipping it left-handed, like we did all those times in practice, he decided to take the ball with two hands and tried to basketball pass it. He ends up fumbling on the 3-yard line, and the other team recovered when it should have been a touchdown. We had the play drawn up perfectly, practiced perfectly and when it came time to execute, our quarterback decided he wanted to turn into John Stockton and bounce-pass the ball with two hands. You just never knew what you were going to get from a rookie quarterback.

Kevin Hogan was the last of my starting quarterbacks. He was a Stanford guy. He was a really good scrambler. He wasn't super-fast, but he was so much more physical than your normal quarterback. He was not afraid to hit people. In 2016, he came in off the bench and rushed for more than 100 yards at Cincinnati. His only start came in 2017, at Houston, the week before my final game. It did not go well. He threw three first-half interceptions and we lost, 33-17.

Another time when things didn't go so well was in 2012. It was the season finale at Pittsburgh. We were down to our third-string quarterback Thad Lewis. Since Thad was our only healthy quarterback, we had to sign a backup for that game. Enter Josh Johnson. He signed on Dec. 26 and we played at Pittsburgh on Dec. 30. We were really gearing up for Thad to make his first-ever start so he got all the reps that week.

Fast forward to the game, and it's the fourth quarter and we were actually making a nice drive down the field toward the scoreboard at Heinz Field. Our left guard goes the wrong way and totally blows the protection. Thad gets decapitated. As he is lying on the field, a guy no one really knew, who had just shown up a couple days earlier, trots onto the field. This new guy gets to the huddle and I say, "Wait a minute, who the hell are you?" He says, "I'm your quarterback." So I ask "What's your name?" "Josh Johnson." I say, "Nice to meet you, Josh, I'm your left tackle Joe Thomas."

Everyone kind of laughed and that broke the tension because it was a pretty big moment in the game. We were down 14 with 1:22 remaining. But we were at the Steelers' 36-yard line so if we get a quick score, we are right back in it.

That is not what happened.

The left guard screwed the protection again, Josh got sacked and fumbled. The Steelers recovered and were able to run out the clock. Josh literally played one play in Cleveland, and it was a sack-fumble.

Another non-starter who played snaps during my time was Charlie Whitehurst. After injuries to RGIII and Josh McCown in consecutive games to start the 2016 season, we needed a backup for Cody Kessler. Enter the ultimate backup quarterback, well at least the ultimate nickname for a backup quarterback — Clipboard Jesus, Charlie Whitehurst. He did not get on the field his first two games, but an injury to Cody at the end of the first half at New England brought Charlie to the huddle. The only thing I remember, besides his long flowing hair, was that he also got injured in the fourth quarter of that game. He finished the game, but he suffered a knee injury and his time with the Browns was over. He was officially a Cleveland Brown for 22 days.

We are getting down to the nitty-gritty because we are now to the college quarterbacks who played wide receiver in the NFL but still played some quarterback for the Browns.

The first is Terrelle Pryor. When he first came to the Browns I had heard some not-so-great stories about what kind of teammate he was, but I found him to be an outstanding teammate. He really put in the work to improve.

He started at quarterback at Ohio State then started at quarterback for the Raiders and for whatever reason that fizzled out. So he converted to receiver and he really put in the work to be a receiver. I was usually one of the last players to leave the building each day, and TP was consistently one of those last guys there with me watching film, asking questions, getting his body right. He gave everything he had to be a great receiver and he ended up putting together a 1,000-yard season.

He never outright said it to me, but I think it was tough for him when he was asked to take snaps at quarterback. We had injuries and were depleted so he came in as kind of a running quarterback who could also throw. He had devoted so much time to becoming a top wide receiver that I think he would have preferred to just stay there.

My most memorable game with him behind center was at Miami in 2016. He took several snaps at quarterback, but not only that, he was at wide receiver on all the other plays. He played 78 of our 82 offensive snaps (95 percent), which is much higher than your typical wide receiver would play. He led the team in receiving with eight receptions for 144 yards, while adding 35 yards passing on five attempts and 21 yards rushing on four attempts. The craziest thing though is that he also played a snap on defense. They put him in to knock down a Hail Mary attempt on the last play of the first half. That is just unheard of, but it's a testament to how much this game meant to him and how much he wanted to win. For that, I loved Terrelle Pryor.

Josh Cribbs is the final player to take snaps at quarterback during my time with the Browns. He was the epitome of a gadget quarterback. He was our wildcat when that craze took over the NFL. He played quarterback at Kent State and joined the Browns as an undrafted free-agent wide receiver/return ace. He was not your typical quarterback. He would get the snap and he would just run around back there until he found a hole to run through. His health be damned, he was going to run through a wall for everyone on that team because he believed that every time he touched the ball he was going to end up in the end zone. That reckless abandonment was part of the reason he was so beloved by Browns fans. That's how he was on kickoff and punt return, too. He would see a hole and just run through it as hard as he could.

From wide receivers to first-round busts to one-start wonders, there were all different types of players who lined up under center during my career. Sure, I would have loved to have some more longevity and health for several of them, but that's not how it played out.

17

THE MIND OF AN OFFENSIVE LINEMAN

"You are among 60 other guys who could all be underwear models ... then there's these 15 fat slobs"

It takes a different mindset to play on the offensive line. You are going to be the biggest guys on the team, but you aren't going to get the spotlight. The skinny guys are the ones who score all the touchdowns. After a score, an offensive lineman's job is to just go to the sideline and get ready to do it again. We don't have choreographed dances for the end zone. We are all business. When we are talked about it usually isn't for something good. It's usually because you just jumped offsides or missed a block and got your quarterback creamed.

As an offensive lineman you are just naturally wired to deflect any attention off yourself. There are very few times in an offensive lineman's life cycle where he likes to have the spotlight on him. It's all about the team. Even when you make a nice block, and the team scores a touchdown, typically, the focus is going to be on the person who scored the touchdown. And that's how you want it as an offensive lineman.

I'm happy that I wasn't a quarterback or running back. I like flying under the radar. I get recognized from time to time, but I imagine it would be a lot worse if I had played a different position.

When you think about it, offensive linemen only have bad stats. We only have pressures, hits, hurries and penalties like false starts or holdings. All those things hurt your team. During a game if your name is mentioned it's typically because one of those bad things happened. The best we can do is give our team a chance to win. We aren't the playmakers. We aren't going to win it, but we can sure as heck lose it.

There's a saying that offensive linemen are like mushrooms, and we are a mushroom society. Mushrooms do their best work when they grow in the dark. Put them in the corner and throw shit on them. That's when they blossom into something beautiful. That's kind of how linemen are. We are put in the shittiest rooms, we get the least amount of appreciation. We only get criticism, only shit.

Sometimes it's like we aren't even part of the team until you are needed. During practice we have our own little corner of the field that no one pays attention to while the other guys are doing 7-on-7. We just push the sled around all day, while the other guys have the cameras in their faces. When things go well, the quarterback gets all the credit. Fans remember the defensive player who had the game-winning interception, but no one remembers the offensive line until you are the one who gives up the game-ending sack. There are two givens for any offensive lineman: You are overworked and underappreciated. The only other people who share in your misery are other offensive linemen, and that helps bring us closer. That helps build a brotherhood.

This is not complaining. This is just how it is at our position. We accept that. To be great at the position you have to embrace that mentality. That's why the mushroom society is something that is embraced by offensive linemen.

Part of what helps build that strong bond is that you are never singled out for doing something good. You share in the misery. There's no glory in being an offensive lineman, and that's what brings you together. Physically you are alike, too. You are among 60 other guys who could all be underwear models. They have these Adonis-looking bodies. Then there's these 15 fat slobs who no one even wants to see in their pajamas much less their underwear. All these things put together makes your bond tight. You share so many commonalities that nobody else on the team does. There's shared misery playing on the offensive line.

There's a saying that the offensive line is the last bus stop on the line before you become a coach. At any other position, if you get fat or slow then you get moved to offensive line, but when you get too fat or too slow for the offensive line, the only place left for you is in coaching.

Most offensive lineman are motivated by the fear of failure. I certainly was. I never wanted to be the reason why we lost or why something bad happened to our team. You never want everyone looking at you, singling you out, saying, "You messed up." It's motivating. We all feel it. That is why there is such camaraderie among offensive linemen. It's a brotherhood. Fear of failure, of letting your teammates down, is one of the best motivators in sports.

We aren't judged by the number of good plays we have. We are judged by the number of bad ones. If a defensive end has one sack, then fans often think, "Wow, he had a great game." It didn't matter what he did for those other 59 snaps. He could have disappeared. For comparison, if an offensive lineman has 58 perfect blocks and gives up two sacks at the end of a game, the media will be wanting to run that guy out of town. The other 58 snaps of pure domination didn't matter. It's always about the number of negative plays.

You must understand that your position's value is measured by the failures you have, not the successes you achieve. At most other positions it's usually about the great play you can make for the team — the sacks, touchdowns, catches — but as a lineman the only time you get noticed is when you do something bad. Everyone who plays at the highest level understands that it is a no-glory position. When things go well, nobody notices you. When things go badly, everybody blames the offensive line. The no-glory aspect of the position is why, I think, a certain type of person is drawn to it and why the brotherhood and fraternity is so strong. You must understand that your value to the team is consistency, being able to just do your job on every play. As a lineman, one bad play is way worse than having five really good plays. Consistency is key.

I think learning the attention to detail that it takes to be good is the hardest part of being an offensive lineman. My fear of failure and letting people down really drove me to be obsessive over details. I was obsessed about not making any mistakes. I wanted to be a perfectionist.

One of my favorite quotes is, "Be the best at everything that doesn't require talent." I took that to heart. There are the obvious things like always showing up on time, having a positive attitude and being coachable. But for me, being prepared was the most important thing I could do to help put me in a position for success, and in turn putting my team in the best position for success.

I became obsessed with film study. Really as linemen, we are slower and fatter than everyone else on the field, so you have to find ways to make up for the difference between you and the guy you are trying to block all day. That happens with technique and film study. You need to know more about him than he knows about himself. Knowing what your man is going to do before he does it allows you to close the athleticism gap between you and the defensive lineman. If you know the move he is going to make before he makes it, that's where film study comes in. What was really important for me was being able to visualize and see myself on the field. I would watch my opponent, come up with a game plan to handle him, and close my eyes and envision myself being on that field beating this guy over and over and over. I would put myself in the shoes of the person who was out there, and that made a huge difference in building confidence throughout the week while preparing for game day. It might be the first time you have faced this person in reality, but really you have faced him in your mind hundreds of times prior. I knew that usually my opponent didn't watch as much film or study nearly as hard as I did so I felt that gave me an advantage.

I tried to have a unique approach for how I was going to face each opponent based on their strengths and weaknesses. When the game started, I would set in on my specific game plan and that guy would have to adjust to how I was playing him. And once you are 20 or so plays in and you have been kicking his ass, his confidence is shot and you have him right where you want him. That was all credit to film study.

My fear of failure and letting people down really drove me to be obsessive over details. I was obsessed about not making mistakes. I wanted to be a perfectionist. Not everyone was as obsessive with film study as I was, but I tried to teach my fellow linemen what I looked for. My favorite sessions were with right tackle Mitchell Schwartz. He joined the team as a second-round pick in 2012, and we spent four seasons together. He was extremely smart, always the smartest on the team, quarterbacks included. That led to Mitch's nickname of the Oracle. He didn't really get the credit he was due for how good he was in Cleveland. He went on to play for Kansas City and made the All-Pro team four times and helped the Chiefs win a Super Bowl. I loved watching film with him. Our weekly sessions were always very productive. We would have an open forum about the guy we were each going up against. We would brainstorm together how to best attack that player. Working together is part of the bond that brings offensive linemen together.

Another lineman I built a great bond with was center Alex Mack. He was a first-round pick in 2009. He was quirky and silly, which meant we got along great. Alex was tough, and I can't emphasize that enough. In 2011, we were having a normal week of practice. It was a Thursday, and we were getting ready to play the Titans at FirstEnergy Stadium. Right in the middle of practice, Alex just starts throwing up. This was before COVID-19 started a global pandemic. Then, if a guy wasn't feeling well, especially a lineman, you just tough it out. We just thought he had the flu or strep throat; our running back Peyton Hillis sat out the previous game with strep throat. Like I said, Alex was tough, and he hadn't missed a snap let alone a game up to that point in his career, so he forged on. He was queasy during the game, but he played all 87 offensive snaps. Monday, when he came to the facility, they took a closer look and realized he had appendicitis and rushed him to Cleveland Clinic. It just so happened that our bye was the next week and Alex was able to recover in time to play the following game and not miss a snap due to his surgery.

Later in his career, he played in the Super Bowl with the Atlanta Falcons. He played every snap of that game — and he broke his leg during the NFC Championship game *two weeks earlier*. He re-broke his fibula, and if it was the regular season, he likely would have missed months-worth of games. But because it was the Super Bowl and just one last game, there was no keeping Alex off the field. He wanted to gut it out and the doctors said he wouldn't do more damage, so he played and he played like Alex always played, like one of the best centers in NFL history. He is one of the toughest players I ever played with. He was a warrior. It would take a lot to keep him out of a game, and unfortunately that happened the first time he broke his fibula.

On Oct. 12, 2014, we were playing the Pittsburgh Steelers at home. About halfway through the second quarter, we were up 14-3 and driving. It was a run play, and after the play I remember seeing him on the ground. It was really hard for me to watch him on the field because he was obviously in a lot of pain. I remember him laying with his face down, slamming his hand on the ground because he was in so much pain. That was tough to watch. They brought the cart out and he was taken to the locker room for X-rays. Alex, being the tough guy that he is, had developed into an iron man at center. He had played 85 straight games and hadn't missed a snap until that injury. His streak was up over 5,000 plays, which is a huge feat. Knowing how much of an iron man he was, I just knew his injury was serious and that he would be out for a while.

We ended up winning 31-10, but it was pretty emotional, for me especially. We had played every snap together for six years. We went through some really tough times together and for him to get hurt and not be able to enjoy us finally putting a whooping on the Steelers made it tougher. He deserved to be out there with us.

I got emotional because being on the offensive line is a brotherhood. We had been through hell together. We, like so many of my other fellow linemen teammates, had built a bond through that hell. A bond that goes beyond the game of football. That's what it's like to be an offensive lineman.

18

THE BEST OFFENSIVE LINE

"We were all such nerds."

I played with almost 50 offensive linemen during my time with the Browns. I played the most games with Alex Mack (101), John Greco (85), Mitchell Schwartz (64), Eric Steinbach (62) and Shawn Lauvao (53). I played the least with Scott Young (1), Martin Wallace (1), Vinston Painter (3), Anthony Fabiano (4), Nat Dorsey (5) and Jonathan Cooper (5). There were plenty of other memorable teammates in between like Hank Fraley (47), Cam Erving (29), Jason Pinkston (25), Seth McKinney (24), Tony Pashos (18), Lennie Friedman (16), Ryan Tucker (13) and Garrett Gilkey (6). These teammates became some of my best friends.

I played with dozens of different offensive-line combinations, but one stands out as clearly the best offensive line I ever played with. That combination came in 2014 with Joel Bitonio at left guard, Alex Mack at center, John Greco at right guard and Mitchell Schwartz at right tackle. We knew we were the best offensive line in the NFL, but at that time no one outside of that room knew. You just don't get recognition when you are on a bad team.

Looking back, the honors and recognition for that group is remarkable. That group currently has combined for 22 Pro Bowl selections and were named to the All-Pro Team 20 times, including eight first-team selections. Joel is the only one still playing, and he's still doing it at an extremely high level, so I expect those numbers to increase as he continues his career.*

---

* Bitonio was the longest-tenured player on the Browns at the end of the 2022 season.

Joel, Mitch, Alex and I were named to an All-Pro team at least three times. Alex and I were even named to the NFL's 2010's All-Decade team. Greco might seem like the outlier in that group since he didn't get any Pro Bowl or All-Pro selections, but he played great football. He just didn't get the recognition because he played on bad teams. Mitch went on to win the Super Bowl with Kansas City, and Alex played in a Super Bowl with Atlanta.

We loved to call Alex the Golden Retriever. That's who he is. He just wanted to please people, and it always showed up on the field. He gave effort on every single play as if it was his last. When he was a rookie, Eric Mangini was our head coach. When he was coach, if someone made a mistake at practice, they would have to run a lap around the field before they could rejoin practice.

As a rookie, Alex would struggle with the snap a little bit, snap it early or late, whatever. So he would have to take a lap each time. Now some guys would take that time to just take a few plays off. There were some defensive linemen like Shaun Rodgers, who might jump offsides on the first play of that practice period, and if they did you just knew they wouldn't be back until that period ended. They were going to take their time with that lap. Not Alex. When he had to do a lap, he would run like he was in the 400 meters at the Olympics. He would sprint around the field so fast that he wouldn't even miss a play. It was amazing how quick he could run that lap and get back in on the very next play, and on that play run 50 yards down the field. That's the way Alex attacked life and football. He set the tempo for how to practice and how to put forth great effort in everything you do. He helped set the standard for our offensive lines. His exuberance was infectious. There's a reason why after Kyle Shanahan left the Browns after 2014 that he signed Alex in Atlanta and made him the highest paid center in football. Then when Kyle went to San Francisco, he brought Alex there. He was a guy you wanted in your locker room. He led by such a great example, and he brought out the best in all his teammates. He always hustled and took every play with a level of seriousness.

We drafted Mitchell out of Cal in 2012, and he was a great addition to the room, especially for me as a tackle. I learned as much from him as any player I played with. He was so cerebral. He looked at things differently than how I did. We would spend a lot of time together just talking about how we saw the game or the player we were going against. Mitchell was one of the surliest guys I played with, too. He was good at diffusing tension at times with his surliness. He just had a way with his humor, self-deprecation and intelligence to keep things light.

Greco is probably one of the most underrated players I ever played with. We traded for him and before he was even solidified as a starter, he was signed to a long contract. This kept him from really hitting the free-agent market in his prime, so he never got that huge high-dollar contract as a free agent. When you are able to sign those big free-agency deals, that's when it starts to open people's eyes, and because he didn't have that, other people didn't really appreciate how great he was. But man, he was like a bulldozer coming off the ball. He could get on an angle and drive a defensive player 3 or 4 yards off the ball. He was as big a part of the reason for the success that we had running the football as any of the other four of us. He had the quickness and technique, and we trusted him so much in that scheme that he didn't need help with the defensive tackle most times. That made him so valuable because we could add that extra assistance to other places. Also, in a room full of pretty good chefs, he took the cake. Everyone was always excited to eat his food. He would bring over meals when people would have babies or other special occasions. John showing up with food always put a bigger smile on my wife's face than when I would walk through the door, that's for sure.

Joel was drafted as a rookie in 2014. He was the rawest as far as technique goes because he played tackle in college. But he was also a true professional right from the start. He was a huge sponge. He was always eager to listen and learn from anything the older guys said. He made improvements not only every game but also every practice. He has built himself into potentially a Hall of Fame guard. He had such a good base of athleticism and power. You would rarely ever see him out of position. He was also a good fit because he was self-deprecating and had a great sense of humor. As a younger player, sometimes it's hard to know where you fit among an offensive line, but he just fit in perfectly in every way. He embraced his role as a young guy on the line, but quickly was playing like a 10-year vet.

I think what makes any offensive line good is the strength of your weakest link. If you have one bad player on the offensive line, defenses will take advantage of it. Everyone must play together and be on the same page. In the zone scheme we ran, one missed block usually results in a 3-yard loss. I think that the fact that all of us, at our worst, were really good helped us perform consistently. We never gave the defense an area to try to exploit to try to shut us down.

One thing we always said in that room was, "Don't be the reason." Don't be the reason we lose. Don't be the reason something bad happens like a mental error or a holding call. We knew the success of not only everyone in that room, but everyone on the offense depended on us laying that foundation. We put a lot of pressure on ourselves to be at our best. We constantly raised the bar for each. You didn't want to be the one holding everyone back.

Obviously, the performance that we put out on the field was unique but so was the fact we had such common interests and were all such nerds. We were nerdy about learning new words. We would all do the same crossword and see who could finish the fastest.

We liked being together. We liked practicing. We liked playing silly games like who could get back to the huddle the fastest. We did stupid stuff that pushed each other to be our best in practice, but we did it in a fun way. We tried to make everything fun or a game. Other lines are good and practice hard, but they might be miserable. We tried to make everything fun. A season can get exhausting, but keeping things light really helped.

We embraced the situation we were in. We never really had to push anyone because we were each in search of perfection. We had such high standards for ourselves in the weight room, in the meeting room and on the practice field. Playing with that group of five guys was very special.

Don't take my word for it. Hear what each of them has to say.

MITCHELL SCHWARTZ

We were all pretty good players. There's that element, but we were also really good friends. We were versatile and could kind of thrive in any system. We could see football the same way. We had that ability to not have to verbalize anything. People talk about the continuity on the o-line and how that's an advantage, it's that non-verbal aspect. We all saw the game the same way, reacted the same way. I didn't want to leave Cleveland in free agency because of that room and those four guys. We loved coming to work every day. It was super fun. We didn't have team success that anyone wanted, but every single day we got to hang out with each other, we got to play together. It was amazing that that was your job. It was a pretty special offensive-line room.

We each elevated everyone else. You didn't want to be the guy who looks like he's not playing hard when Alex is chasing guys 30 yards down the field. There were little things where you would feed off each other's energy or physicality. You didn't want to let each other down.

Every attribute you could want in an offensive lineman, Joe was the best I have ever seen: The athleticism, flexibility, awareness, anticipation, play strength. The few times he did get beat, the recovery to then not actually get beat. He's the best I've ever seen at every single one of those. For most people it takes a lot of reps and a lot of practice to ingrain something into muscle memory. For him, he could just tell himself, "Do this with your footwork," and his body will react to it and do it properly. It was insane. Basically, whatever he wanted to do he could do correctly the first time.

I tell this story to help people conceptualize how good Joe was. There was a game in Green Bay in 2013, and it was raining. It was later in the game. We were all on the bench kind of looking at each other and comparing our mud stains and how dirty we were. We get to Joe and he's completely clean. We were, "How do you have no mud on you?" He looks down and goes, "Oh, I guess I just haven't been on the ground yet today." He can play left tackle, in the rain and mud in Green Bay, and just not fall on the ground ever. He's that good that he can just make it look that easy.

He is just a good dude, too. Everybody loves him. He treats people well. On top of that, he's a first-ballot Hall of Famer. There are high-level players who are dicks and others who just aren't very nice and he, for all his success, stayed a good dude. He has that gregarious demeanor where he's fun-loving. When he gets animated, he gets loud and super into things. I joke that he's Mr. Hyperbole because when he gets in one of those moods, he makes everything seem like the most hyperbolic statement of all time. That was always funny to me because I am more of a "Well technically" kind of guy.

In regard to the snap streak, I had a good streak there for a while, too. I was talking to Joe one time, and I told him that I would really like to pass his streak. I mean he has every other fucking award, it would be nice to have one thing that I could be known for because he's already known for 18 other things.

Obviously, there's a luck factor that you can play 10 and a half years without missing a snap. Alex had a snap streak and then 800 pounds fell on his leg at the wrong angle and his streak was over. In college, I broke a shoelace and had to miss one single play that entire season due to a shoe malfunction.

There's also the skill element of taking care of your body. Joe was big on stretching, not so much on offseason workouts. There's also the element that he's just a tough dude. I'm sure he played through things that maybe other guys wouldn't have played through. That's a testament to his toughness and his ability to push through those kinds of things.

I got lucky that my snap streak became a thing. It was because

Joe and Alex had snap streaks. There's a story from my third year where the coaches tried to send in a backup for Joe and he sent him back to the sideline because the coaches didn't know about his streak. When we got back to the sideline our o-line coach Andy Moeller asked what was going on. Joe said he had a snap streak. He turns to me and asks to take me out, and I said no because it had been two and a half seasons for me, and I haven't missed a snap, so I preferred to stay in. Then Moeller says, "This is the first time in my entire career that I've tried to pull guys at the end of a game and no one wants to come out." I don't know if I would have had the wherewithal to not come out if Joe didn't have a snap streak. I got lucky that he and Alex had their streaks and I could piggyback off the awareness I otherwise wouldn't have had, especially that early in my career. If Joe and Alex were protecting their streaks then I wanted to protect my much smaller one, too.

JOHN GRECO

We were extremely competitive in that room. We didn't have a lot of success as a team, but I thought we had some pretty good offensive lines, including that 2014 one, and it all started with Joe.

It was such a good group. We were competitive amongst one another. Everyone understood there were unique challenges surrounding the team as a whole and that we could only do so much to help us win games. Our mindset was that if we take care of business, things will sort themselves out. We weren't winning games for the team, but we also weren't the reason why we were losing. We were so dialed into being the best unit. The mission was clear, and we understood what it took to be great and we did everything we could to do that.

I've played on o-lines where you had to dumb it down to the point where you have to say the most obvious things to the guy next to you to make sure he knows what he is doing. That year there was pretty much no communication needed because of the level of trust we had in each other. We knew the guy next to you would be in the right place at the right time and do what they were supposed to do. We worked as one. Every day was about trying to be better. We became perfectionists, and it was so fun.

Joe was the leader. As far as the grade sheets go, I saw him play perfect games. It got lost in the wash because the Browns weren't winning, but in our room, at least we could hold our heads up high and be proud about what we were putting out on the field. It all started at the top with him. If you made a mistake or tried to cut corners, he held you accountable. I think that made us all better.

He's such a technician on the field. If you watched him take 5,000 pass sets, I bet 98 percent of them would look the exact same. That's so important at that position. It doesn't matter who he is lining up against because he has a plan and he sticks to it.

Playing with him and seeing the focus and attention to detail, the preparation that he did, it was an eye-opener for me. I mean this guy, who has all the skill, is still putting in serious amount of work in preparation. It showed that his craft was really important to him. I saw that, and that ultimately made me a better player.

It's rare when a pinnacle guy on your team, a cornerstone of the franchise, can lead so well on and off the field. Not everyone is like that.

You could see what made him so great with his preparation and attention to detail and how serious he took his job. That kind of thing automatically raises the bar and expectations in your position room. If you don't elevate yourself to that level, you get left behind really quick. It just happened naturally.

I have been around guys who would get up in front of the team and preach and it's like, "How are you going to tell me to do that when you don't even do that?" What made Joe one of the best leaders I've been around is because he automatically had that respect factor because he did it the right way on and off the field.

When I was drafted by the Rams, I played with Orlando Pace. Growing up in Ohio, his name was synonymous with the pinnacle of offensive-line play, and in particular the tackle position. He went to Ohio State, and I grew up in Ohio so I wanted to be like him.

Joe and I were around the same age so I was very well aware of his success at Wisconsin and early in his NFL career. When I was traded to the Browns in 2011, I was really excited because I was leaving one Hall of Fame tackle to another future Hall of Fame tackle. I was excited to meet him and I knew the team had some seriously good players with Joe and Alex Mack.

Joe and I hit it off right away. The one thing about Joe is that he is always busting balls. He would always poke at you and find a way to rip on you, but always in a fun manner and with a laugh. I picked up on that right away.

A good testament to that is during the offseason prior to that 2014 season, I got married. I went on my honeymoon, and I showed up to offseason workouts overweight. That year was one of the hardest offseason conditioning programs that we had. I was trying to cut my weight. The team would go through a full workout and then I had to do extra. Joe being Joe, always made it a point to walk by the six to eight of us guys who had to do that extra conditioning. I remember busting my ass on the stationary bike after a tough workout and Joe made sure to walk by and laugh at us. He knew we were miserable and would just pile on. He would come over and say, "Hey, what are you guys doing?" just because he knew we were at our boiling point, me in particular. But it was always in good fun. Joe always found a way to keep things fun.

Playing with Joe, I found out right away what it took to be a professional. My time in Cleveland were my best years individually, and a lot of that had to do with trying to emulate Joe.

JOEL BITONIO

It was a blast playing with those guys. I played tackle in college so when I came in and they said, "You're going to play guard next to Joe Thomas" I was, "OK, this is pretty special." I knew I was going to try to learn as much as I could from him. I was at left guard between Joe and Alex. Alex is one of the best centers of his generation and Joe is arguably one of the best tackles, ever. It was a special opportunity for a rookie, who has never played guard before, to come in and get to play between those two.

When I first got there for the first OTA practice, I had no idea what the plan was. They told me, "You are rolling with the ones today." I wasn't expecting that yet, but they just wanted to throw me in the fire, I guess. I remember seeing Joe and thinking, "Everyone who I have ever talked to about the Browns told me that this guy was the best, that he was the man." So I am out there on my first play and my first thought — besides "Don't mess up the play" — was "Don't step on this guy's foot or get in his way." He's on a Hall of Fame trajectory and hasn't missed a snap. I didn't want to be the guy to trip him or step on his foot. I was panicked to just not get in his way that first day. But it all worked out.

Joe was a consummate professional. I remember one of my first meetings, it was a medical meeting. Joe had probably sat through a meeting like this at the start of every one of his seasons. But I noticed he had his notebook and pencil out and was taking notes. I asked him, "What are you taking notes on?" He said, "Whenever someone is up there talking, no matter who it is, I always try to write something down because you can always learn something from anybody who's up there." I thought that showed such respect for the team and the professionalism he had for his craft. That is something that I have taken into my game and used myself.

Besides the mentorship, he just internally pushed me to be a better player because I didn't want to let him down. I don't want to be the weak link next to him. It pushed me to try to up my game every chance I had.

It was a fun room to be in, and I didn't know any better. It was my first taste of an NFL o-line room. Alex and Mitch both went to Cal, so they were West Coast guys. Then you had a Wisconsin and a Toledo guy. It was just a good mix. There was a lot of humor, and we were never too tight.

It all started at the top with Joe obviously, the best left tackle in football. Then down the line, Alex Mack was a great center who played the game the right way. He always played so hard and it made the group think, "I want to play hard like him." John Greco was there, and now looking back from my experience playing in the league, he was criminally underrated in his career. He was a very strong starting guard for the Browns for five or six years. Mitch was a very impressive player who was still pretty young in his career. In Cleveland, there was kind of this narrative by media and fans that he wasn't as good a tackle as Joe was, but c'mon — nobody was as good as Joe. Mitch ended up getting several All-Pros and won a Super Bowl. I was the last guy in that group, and I knew I was just going to play hard. When you put us five together in Kyle Shanahan's wide-zone play-action offense, it let us do our best work.

I was the rookie in the room. They had been around, so they knew what they wanted when it came to performing rookie duties like getting coffee or sunflower seeds. If I got the wrong size sunflower seeds, I'd have to hear about it. Being the only rookie, I was certainly picked on a bit and they all got a good laugh at my expense at times.

There was such a high standard of work that it raised everyone else's standard in that room, backups included and even the coaching staff. It started with self-accountability. The guys just wanted to be great players and had their own standard of excellence.

If you look at Joe's resume with all the All-Pros, Pro Bowls, you see why he was a lock for the Hall of Fame. But if you actually watch the tape and see what he did in pass protecting and run blocking, wow. The number of quarterbacks he protected at such an elite level, it's no easy task. There are guys who have the same quarterback for their whole career and Joe was playing with three or four quarterbacks a season and he kept that level of excellence. When at times everything around him was crumbling, he was the standard. You knew you could always count on Joe Thomas to be there on Sunday. And not just be there, but also perform at an extremely high level. Win, lose or draw he always put his best effort out there.

ALEX MACK

To me, it wasn't even about the talent, which was apparent, but it was just such a good group of guys. We were all friends. Four of us overlapped for a long time with the Browns. There was a lot of turnover in Cleveland and we were lucky that the new coaches saw the value in keeping us around. We had a great o-line room. Everyone was a good worker.

We had a ton of different coordinators. We were taught all these different techniques and schemes. We were exposed to a huge variety of possibilities, so we were able to figure out what worked best for us. When Kyle showed up in 2014 with the outside zone stuff, we already had a great knowledge and background with each other.

Oddly enough though, the biggest part of why we were good would be that our team was bad. Every week we were all dedicated and worked hard. We would play pretty good ball, but we would lose the game. So then you would have to take a look in the mirror and say, "Well you didn't play perfectly so you have to do better." It was never good enough, so we always tried to be better and improve. I think that enabled us to never get complacent and keep striving to be better.

We got lucky to have that level of talent in the same room. We were all physically gifted, smart, and hardworking guys. Offensive linemen always prefer to run the ball because you can control so much more of the game. If you move your man and open running lanes, you're going to have success. Pass protection is far more difficult and fickle. You don't always know where the QB is, especially when you have played with so many different ones. If you do give great protection, you're still relying on the QB to throw it to the right guy, and the right guy to catch it. There are a few games that come to mind where we took over by just running the ball.

We were all just kind of nerdy dudes, too. We did word of the day when we had to go out to practice early to warm up and do more o-line drills than actual practice gave time for. We got into crosswords one year. But you spent a lot of time together. It's bus rides, plane rides, before and after practices, time in the weight room — you were constantly around these people and for us to be able to enjoy each other so much was lucky.

One year our head o-line coach had to be suspended for the season, right at the first day of the season, and that really cemented what kind of group we had. We had all done so much together and knew how to get the job done. The assistant o-line coach who had to step up and coach us that year really saw that we knew what we were doing and gave us a lot of free rein to decide how we wanted to solve problems every week. Mitch's encyclopedic memory came in handy because he would remember exactly how we did things two or three years previously. It was so much fun to take ownership of the offensive-line position as a collective group.

We were all big foodies, too. Obviously, we all liked eating, but we also liked cooking. One year Colt McCoy got all the linemen Big Green Egg grills, and we would have big barbecues together. Numerous times a year we would do a big potluck and guys would come over to share whatever they made.

You never wanted to miss a game or even miss a play because

you liked the guy next to you. You always wanted to do your job but also do what you could to help the guy next to you.

I really enjoyed those guys and was so happy about my time together. We weren't successful. We didn't always win games, but I have such fond memories of my time in Cleveland because of the people I spent it with.

19

ONE LAST VICTORY

"I don't think anyone really knew how tough it was actually going to be."

Being on a bad NFL team is miserable. It is particularly miserable at the end of the season. At that point, everyone is trying to save their own job. They know change is in store. Lots of people will be fired. That's the reality of this business. Everyone is miserable. The players know they may get cut. The media is on you to explain why things have gone sour. Fans are irate. It's not fun.

When things are going bad, which happened a lot during my playing days, the main thing is keeping the main thing the main thing. Yes, you read that right. That means you focus on doing your job. You do your job and trust that man next to you will do his. You have to focus on that play, that day. Just worry about your own house. You can't focus on all the external noise.

We had some rough seasons during my time with the Browns, and 2016 was one of the worst. It was Hue Jackson's first year as head coach. To say we had a young team would be an understatement. During the offseason we let multiple starters leave via free agency, including center Alex Mack, right tackle Mitchell Schwartz, wide receiver Travis Benjamin and defensive back Tashaun Gipson. Alex had been selected to multiple Pro Bowls. Mitch was widely considered the best right tackle in the league. Travis was coming off nearly a 1,000-yard season and set numerous team records as a returner. Tashaun was among the league leaders in interceptions and was a Pro Bowler. To see those guys leave plus other key contributors like linebacker Craig Robertson and special-teams ace Johnson Bademosi leave was tough.

It hurt more because Alex and Mitch were close friends of mine. We spent so much time together and developed a real bond. We had been together for years. They were my best friends on the team, but they were also great players and they just walked out the door and signed with other teams. It was tough because I knew the Cleveland Browns got worse.

How does a team get to the point where many key players are just walking out the door? It comes from the constant change in coaching and management. One important thing a franchise must do is be able to identify talent early in their career. When you draft someone, you identify their talent and re-sign them before they get to free agency. It sounds so easy, but when a new coach or general manager comes in, they want to learn their players. They want to see what they inherited. They need to see what everyone can do. They want to learn how they fit in their system before they re-sign anyone. If you keep changing coaches and management every year or every other year, then the guys who should have been identified and re-signed early in their career get to free agency and have the opportunity to leave. That's why having stability at the top of an organization is so important. If that happens then they can draft a player, identify who was a hit and re-sign them before they get to free agency. Once you get to free agency all it takes is one team to fall in love and throw a big number at him, then there is nothing you can do. Now all the effort and energy you put into developing a young player into a great NFL player is gone.

You also have people who say, "Well you were 3-13 with those guys, you can be 3-13 without them." But if you want to be better than 3-13, you have to keep your good players. That is just the way it goes. You can't keep getting rid of good players and think you are going to get better.

After those guys left in free agency, we purged our roster even more. Vets like wide receiver Brian Hartline, linebacker Paul Kruger and defensive back Donte Whitner also were let go in efforts to make our team younger. The decision was made to tear the foundation of the team down to the studs and rebuild with young players. They wanted to build a core, a young nucleus of players with the emphasis on "young."

When the draft came around we made several trades and ended up with 14 draft picks. It's a seven-round draft and we ended up with 14 players. So we basically had two drafts in one year.

Now, when you've spent draft equity on a player, you don't want to let that player leave before you can really see what they can do. So we kept all 14 players during final roster cuts before the season. I don't know if we were the youngest team in NFL history, but if not, we had to be darn close.

The truth is that guys don't know what they don't know at that age. It's tough when you go into a game and most of your starters are first- or second-year players and you are playing against teams that have had core guys together for five or six years. It puts you behind the eight ball. In the NFL, the most basic thing you do is at a calculus level. Everything is advanced. We brought in 14 kindergartners to a calculus class. I wasn't a math major, but I know when more than 25 percent of your roster is rookies you are in for some growing pains. Even with growing pains expected, I don't think anyone really knew how tough it was actually going to be.

We started 0-14 — the worst start in team history at the time. We had three different starting quarterbacks in each of the first three games, but it wasn't like we were getting blown out. During our home opener, we jumped out to a 20-0 lead against our divisional rival Baltimore Ravens, but they scored 25 straight to steal the win. The next week, our kicker got hurt at a Friday walk-through practice. Practice injuries were common that week as we also lost our first-round pick to a broken hand during practice. So we were without a kicker and had to sign a free agent the day before the game in Miami. The new guy missed three field goals that game, including a potential game-winner with the score tied as time expired. We lost in overtime.

As the losses mounted and we are sitting at 0-9, then 0-10, then

0-11, things looked dim. I am sure you have heard NFL players say the cliché that you only focus on the next game and that is true. Win or lose, the next day you block out what happened and focus strictly on the next game. You never want to get too up or too down or things will weigh on you.

As the season went on you could clearly see the young guys playing better than they had at the beginning of the season. We were playing as a team. We had some injuries to some key players, but there was a real tight bond being forged with a real stick-to-it-ness attitude. We were resilient. There was a lot of pride in that locker room. I had seen earlier in my career that when things were going south toward the end of a season, players would be making plans for the offseason. They lost focus. They didn't seem to care. I did not see that in this team. There was no quit.

We were 0-14 and hosting the San Diego Chargers at home on Christmas Eve and we finally came together and played a complete team game that resulted in our lone win of the season. I remember all three phases played a crucial role in the victory. The Pierogi Prince of Parma, Jamie Meder, a kid who grew up a Browns fan and embodied the toughness of the city, blocked a field goal late in the fourth quarter to maintain a 20-17 lead. The Chargers got the ball back and drove down the field and attempted a game-tying field goal as time expired. After the kick sailed wide right, tears sailed down my face.

I didn't expect it to be emotional, but I think that's one of the beautiful things about the game of football. Sometimes you're just overcome with emotion and it's totally unexpected, but I think it's a great thing. Football is the ultimate team game. You're putting aside any personal ambitions for the good of the team and everyone pulled together and we got that first victory. I didn't know it at the time, but it would be my last NFL victory.

The game ended, and I was on the field looking for people to hug. I was really happy. It was a genuine feeling of joy. Our PR guy grabbed me and told me I needed to do the on-field interview with CBS. I must have been the first lineman in league history to do the postgame interview. It's usually the starting quarterback, but Robert Griffin suffered a concussion during the game and wasn't able to do media so I think they just said they would take whoever they could get and they got me. I'm sure the ratings went through the roof for that one.

Because of the interview, I was one of the last people off the field, and as I entered the locker room our head coach Hue Jackson had already started his postgame speech. The team was huddled around him and he called me right into the middle. Things got emotional. We were all so happy. The tears kept coming.

A video went up where you can see me sobbing postgame, so I certainly got a healthy dose of teasing from my friends. I would have expected nothing less. Everyone was just so overcome in the moment. When you look back at it, you feel a bit silly crying over 1-14 as your record, but I think with all that we went through and as much as we put in every single day, it was such a relief to get that win. It's a moment I will never forget.

I kept telling myself, "You shouldn't be this happy. This is not that big of a deal. We just won a game and it doesn't even matter." But it definitely felt like it was more than just a win. You don't want to say it was like our Super Bowl, but it really was. Everyone was excited — players, coaches, you could feel it in the stadium with the fans. The season didn't go our way, but we battled every week. We didn't pack it in. We stayed the course and bought in. I couldn't have been prouder in that moment. To be honest, part of the reason the team didn't quit on that season was because we were so young. Everyone had something to prove. That's one of the benefits of being young and dumb.

I wish we had more wins, but that being my final one is something I'll always cherish.

20

THE SNAP STREAK

"I'm just a guy who shows up and does his job every day."

It started with my first play, a nervous rookie making his NFL debut. That turned into my first game, a blowout loss to the Steelers. That turned into my rookie season, my only winning season in the NFL. Then it just kept adding up, play after play, season after season. I always wanted to do everything I could do to help my team win. To me, that meant always staying on the field. To be there for the people who needed you. I learned at a young age, you stay on the field until you can't. My mom and dad instilled in me that you just get up and you go to work and you don't make a big deal about it.

There were aches and pains, but I was raised to fight through the pain. You don't let your body tell you that you can't get up and play another play. You don't let your mind tell you those things. You just keep going so that's what I did.

I always thought, they hired me to do a job and that job requires me to get my butt up, get back to the huddle, get the next play and go do it again. And I'll keep doing that until I physically can't get up or they tell me you're not good enough to be out there anymore. So I just kept getting up.

Around my fifth or sixth season is when I actually took notice. I was talking with Alex Mack and Mitchell Schwartz and none of us had missed a snap the year before. As we talked through it, I realized I didn't miss one from the year before that or the year before that and so on. I thought that was a pretty neat thing so I decided, I want to keep this thing going as long as I could and not go out of the game for a hangnail or something. It became a point of pride.

Let's be real, I know having a streak like that takes a lot of luck. In the NFL when there is an injury and the trainers come on the field to tend to you, you must sit out the next play regardless of how you feel. You also don't just miss plays due to injuries — your shoe could burst open, jersey rip in half, face mask break, lose a contact lens or any number of minor missteps to force you off the field for a play or two. But I got lucky, so I just kept going to work and not making a big deal about it.

Now there were a couple instances where my streak almost ended. One was the season finale in 2013. We were playing at Pittsburgh. It was a meaningless game. We were out of the playoffs and they were, too. It ended up being Rob Chudzinski's final game as head coach.

I will admit it was the dumbest injury I have ever gotten. I was dealing with some back spasms at the time, so I needed to keep my back loose and continuously stretch. I lifted my leg across the other, placing my ankle atop the opposite knee. I bent down with force, probably too much force because I heard a pop in my knee. I instantly knew something was wrong. I could walk, gingerly, and it felt OK to just stand on so I figured I would just play the next play and see what happens. I was worried I wouldn't be able to do my job, but I made it through the play. At that point, it is what it is, and you aren't going to make it worse, so I was able to limp through the rest of the game, a game we lost 20-7.

That's when they took me to get an MRI and I found out it was a pretty significant injury. I tore my lateral collateral ligament (LCL), a grade 2 tear. I needed four to six weeks to let that heal. Luckily, it was the last game of the season or I would have been forced to miss a few games.

Another time the streak was in jeopardy was in 2014. Mike Pettine was our head coach. We were actually blowing out the Steelers. Unfortunately, it was usually the other way around most of my career. It was Week 6 and we were at home. We jumped out on them pretty good. It was 21-3 at halftime and later 31-3 in the fourth quarter. I'm out on the field enjoying this rare feeling of a blowout win when I look over and I see my backup Vinston Painter come trotting onto the field.

Painter was a sixth-round pick by the Broncos out of Virginia Tech in 2013. He spent some time on their practice squad but didn't appear in any games his rookie year. The Browns signed him in 2014 and he was making his NFL debut that week.

As I saw him running on the field, I started looking around wondering what he was doing. Did someone else get hurt and I didn't see it? He comes right up to me and says, "Hey Joe, I got you."

I say: "You don't got me. Get the fuck out of here."

The poor guy didn't know what to do. He stood there bewildered for a second or two. So he started to ask the other guys on the line if he could sub in for them and they all told him no. He turned around and ran back to the sideline with his tail between his legs. I felt bad because he was just doing what the coaches told him to do. I knew about my streak and we were actually winning so there was no way I was willingly just going to take myself out and have it come to an end. I was going to enjoy this. Meanwhile the coaches are on the sidelines wondering what was going on because they were trying to sub out some of the veteran players to avoid a late-game injury.

Later they found out that I hadn't missed a snap in my career. It was Mike Pettine's first year as head coach, and he didn't know that I had never missed a snap. We seemed to have new coaches every year or two and I never introduced myself as, "Hi, I'm Joe Thomas and I've never missed a snap." It wasn't something that was really talked about at that point, but I knew about it, so I kept going. I would continue to just go to work and not make a big deal out of it.

The snaps just kept adding up until a milestone approached: 10,000 was on the horizon. All of a sudden, the "not make a big deal out of it" part was out of my hands. I never wanted the attention on me, though. I never wanted people to treat me like a star. I am an offensive lineman. I always wanted the attention to be on my teammates. I entered the second week of the 2017 season with 9,996 consecutive snaps, and the media went to town. Everyone wanted to talk about it. I tried to tell them it wasn't a big deal. I'm just a guy who shows up and does his job every day.

The focus was on me and I didn't like it. I did read an ESPN story where they had quotes from a player on each side of the ball talking about my streak. It was two players I have so much respect for. One was former NFL Defensive Player of the Year and seven-time Pro Bowler Terrell Suggs and the other was some guy who played quarterback named Tom Brady.

Suggs had said: "Damn. That is legit. That is pretty amazing, especially in this league. It is a physical league for his position. That is a pretty awesome milestone, accomplishment."

And Brady said: "It's incredible. For him to do it, he's obviously had a lot of regimes and he's been such a remarkable player. A consistent elite performer. He's been to so many Pro Bowls, came out really highly touted, and he's just played at a Pro Bowl level almost every single year. That's a tough position to play all those snaps. But he does it. It's really a credit to him."

I thought that was really cool, but for the first time I started to feel a little bit of pressure heading into that game. I hoped I didn't get rolled up on during the first three plays.

The game was in Baltimore and we got the ball first. I thought, "Good, let's get this out of the way early." And then we went three and out, which brought out our punt team and sent me to the sidelines at 9,999. When we got the ball back, we were backed up at our 9-yard line. It was a simple handoff, a 9-yard run over the right guard by Isaiah Crowell. I was happy the game was in Baltimore because there was no fanfare. No in-game announcement. I think that could have been cool for the fans if it was in Cleveland, but I didn't want any of that. I was able to get back to the huddle, get the next play and do it again. I went about my business, and the game ended with a 24-10 loss.

What came after the game was a truly humbling experience. So many people reached out to congratulate me.

Commissioner Roget Goodell tweeted, "Congrats @joethomas73 on your 10,000+ consecutive snap streak. There's no questioning your dedication & your excellence on and off the field."

Fellow Wisconsin mate J.J. Watt tweeted, "10,000 consecutive snaps. That's unbelievable. Hats off to you good sir, @joethomas73."

And the King LeBron James tweeted, "Unbelievable @joethomas73!! 10k consecutive snaps played! Playing in the trenches too! Crazy man! Congrats big fella!!"

It really put me at a loss for words. I was so humbled by the outpouring of respect that people showed. I was always just a guy who just wanted to work and not make a big deal about it. I just wanted to do my part to help the team win. The spotlight was on me, and it was tough at times, but in reality the spotlight was on everyone who helped me along the way. All of my teammates, coaches, family and friends.

People were comparing me to Cal Ripken. I remember when he broke the consecutive-games-played record. He said he was happy to get it over with so people could stop talking about it. He could just focus on baseball. I kind of felt the same way as he did. I was happy I got to 10,000 straight and then we were able to move on and take the attention off me and put it back where it should be — on my teammates.

And that's exactly what happened, and I just kept playing. Snap after snap until a home game against the Titans on Oct. 22, 2017. It was the third quarter, we were trailing 6-3, but putting a drive together. It was first-and-10 at the Tennessee 29-yard line. The play was 13 Wilson. Every team has that play, it's a weak-side run from the shotgun. It ended up being a 3-yard run by Duke Johnson. It's a routine play that I have done a million times. I went to block Brian Orakpo and toward the end of the play I just felt something unnatural in my arm. I knew what happened. I tore my left triceps. I could feel the tendon detach from elbow and it rolled up into my mid-triceps. It was a creepy feeling and it was a sharp, stabbing pain.

I had no function in my left arm. I knew right away that I wasn't going to be able to keep playing. I think you can play with about 30 to 40 percent function in one arm, but when you have no function, especially your left arm when you are a left tackle, it is impossible to block an edge-rusher with only one hand. It was a freak injury. I was blocking guys for so many years with that one arm with the same motion, and over time my tendon just broke down.

And just like that, the streak ended at 10,363 consecutive plays. The NFL doesn't have official records for consecutive plays but for comparison sake, after my injury my former teammate Mitchell Schwartz, who was with the Chiefs at the time, became the new NFL leader with 5,536 consecutive snaps played. His streak was later snapped at 7,894 following a knee injury. Alex Mack also ran his consecutive-snaps streak to 5,279 before breaking his leg.

My streak wasn't what was on my mind, though. I wanted to know the severity of the injury and if I would be able to get back out there with my teammates. It was kind of an out-of-body experience. The trainers came out and they took me to the injury tent. I wasn't able to push at all and I knew that wasn't good. It was a terrible feeling knowing that my team was out there and all I could do was watch. I wasn't able to help them.

They took me to the locker room for more tests and X-rays. My wife, Annie, was able to meet me there. I had to watch the game on a TV as we came back and took the Titans to overtime but ended up losing 12-9. I was so proud of how the team fought, but I wished I was able to help more.

Then the bad news came. The MRI on Monday confirmed the injury would be season-ending and I would need surgery to reattach the tendon. They told me it would be six to nine months for a full recovery. My surgery was set for Tuesday morning.

It was a crazy two-day span. It started as a normal game. It was my 167th straight game and it ended up being my last. I missed my first play and then missed the rest of the season. It was a helpless feeling.

Right before surgery, I wasn't upset though. I thought how glad I was that my tendon didn't snap on play 9,996. I was proud that I was able to hit that 10,000 mark and be there for my team play after play, game after game, year after year. Injuries happen in the NFL all the time, and I was able to avoid a major one for 10 and a half years. I knew how lucky I was. I didn't take a single one of those 10,363 snaps for granted. I just wanted to give my all every time, every play and I was able to do that for my entire career.

POSTSCRIPTS

THE END AND NEW BEGINNINGS

Joe Thomas' NFL career lasted almost four times that of the average NFL player.

The end of his career was already in the back of his mind when Thomas suited up for a game against Tennessee on Oct. 22, 2017. In the third quarter, as he was blocking Brian Orakpo, he suddenly grabbed his left arm and fell, writhing in pain.

Thomas' offensive-line mate Joel Bitonio told Nate Ulrich of the Akron Beacon Journal: "It's really been unbelievable what he's done with his career and to see a guy like that, I kind of thought for a second he was unbreakable almost, like nothing could go wrong with him. To see him go down, you kind of realized he was a mortal among us."

In the game, Thomas had privately told Bitonio his elbow was bothering him, that he couldn't push against a defender. On the block against Orakpo, he tore his left triceps. The triceps allow a person to extend the forearm at the elbow joint. Thomas wrote in a piece for Sports Illustrated he could feel the tendon roll up in his arm.

Coach Hue Jackson sent in Spencer Drango to replace him. Surgery would follow.

When it came to making a decision regarding retirement, Thomas wanted to make sure it was the right time, one he could live with.

"You know, obviously, we've seen a lot of guys retire and unre-tire. And I knew that I didn't want that to be me. And so I think it was an easy decision to retire. But it made it harder knowing that it was sort of a finality. It was sort of like the end of my football life."

But dealing with a painful knee, not being able to separate the pain "from the joy of being an NFL player," led him to decide to retire.

After more than a decade of Browns fans seeing Joe Thomas lumber up to the left side of the offensive line as No. 73, an era ended. It had begun with Thomas cracking the starting lineup on Sept. 9, 2007, against Pittsburgh, almost 3,700 days earlier.*

It might surprise fans to know it wasn't the triceps but his knee that was on his mind before the game.

"It's hard to say, but I think I would have retired after that season anyway. I mean, the memories I have in my head of the last year is just like dragging my leg down the hallway. From meeting room to meeting room, pretty much on crutches. Getting my knee drained every week, getting injected with cortisone and Euflexxa, which is like a hyaluronic acid, and the pills, the anti-inflammatories, and then the painkillers on game day just to get out there. And it was a routine that was working, but it was just miserable. And I knew that it was not something that was sustainable for the long run."

After retiring, Thomas slimmed down. It is imperative that players, especially linemen who are used to taking in a lot of calories during their career (a wide range would be 3,500 to 8,000 daily), change their diet in retirement. Otherwise, there are knee replacements waiting to happen, not to mention other serious health concerns. With the knowledge of nutrition and physiology that athletes possess nowadays, it is not a surprise that post-career weight loss has become a thing. The poster child for this might be

---

* The trivia question of who Thomas replaced is an interesting one—a game of musical chairs in shoulder pads: Kevin Shaffer, Cleveland's left tackle in 2006, moved to right tackle in 2007. Eric Steinbach was signed as a free agent and played left guard in 2007, his first year with Cleveland. Joe Andruzzi, left guard in 2006, was cut. Shaffer played through 2008 with the Browns, then two seasons with Chicago before hanging it up. What happened to Andruzzi? He was released weeks after Thomas signed. It would be a horrible month for Andruzzi. Not long after being released, he was about to board a flight for an NFL team visit, hoping to extend his career, but was notified by a doctor that a large mass was discovered on his colon. The mass, he was told, was expected to double in size — in 24 hours. He was diagnosed with stage-4 cancer. After aggressive chemotherapy, he survived. In 2013, Andruzzi was one of the people on the site of the tragic Boston Marathon bombing, where he helped carry victims to safety.

former Pittsburgh Steelers lineman Alan Faneca, who dropped his diet to 1,800 calories per day, lost 100 pounds, and ran a marathon. In 2021, he was inducted into the Hall of Fame after a brilliant career. Marshal Yanda, who played 13 seasons for Baltimore, slashed his daily caloric intake from 6,000 to 2,200 and immersed himself in exercise. Thomas did, too. The weight loss began almost immediately.

One thing that those close to Thomas point out is that he always was about more than football. He has other interests. He soaks up knowledge. That trait serves athletes especially after their careers end. Most NFL players retire in their 20s. Football might be everything for them until that point, but without interests, family life or business diversions, that life can be an empty, lonely road.

Jeff Gryzwa, a science teacher at Brookfield Central, knows firsthand about Thomas and the outdoors. Gryzwa had him as a senior in ecology class, which he extended for a year as an independent study because of Thomas' love of the environment.* Gryzwa has been fishing with Thomas multiple times, bluegill to bass. They also hunted turkey together.

"The guy," Gryzwa said, "is a true outdoorsman." He recalled that Thomas used to go to the Boundary Waters Canoe Area Wilderness in northern Minnesota / Canada. It's a leave-no-trace-behind-you area. So visitors must portage canoes and kayaks and live off of the land as much as possible, he said. As the story goes, Thomas went on a trip with a church group. Everyone brought food. Everyone, that is, except Thomas. He brought his fishing pole and a knife, Gryzwa said.

"And that was it."

Despite his love for the environment, Thomas did have a minor bureaucratic mishap involving the Division of Natural Resources in 2014.

Thomas had purchased farmland that included some dilapi-

---

* The environment isn't the only thing Thomas loved. Before nutrition became a priority for him, he loved candy. Science teacher Jeff Gryzwa said Thomas would bring a two- or three-pound bag of mixed candy to class. What he didn't love? Sharing. "He would just sit and eat the whole thing," Gryzwa said.

dated buildings. The previous owners had a choice of selling to the public — the Division of Natural Resources — or to a private party, like Thomas. Thomas had contacted the U.S. Fish and Wildlife Service and the nonprofit Ducks Unlimited to come up with a plan to help improve the property for wildlife, including ducks, deer and turkeys. They discussed the creation of ponds and restoring wetlands. The officials then contacted the Department of Natural Resources, who said permits were required for some of the work. Thomas hired a contractor and a recycler to work on the buildings, grade the property and get rid of the trash piles. Unbeknownst to Thomas, a couple of permits were not obtained. According to Thomas, one local official with another organization — upset that the land did not go to the public — took a letter that had been sent to Thomas warning him of potential fines because of the permit issue and leaked it to the media.

But the letter was sent while Thomas was in the middle of football season, so he was blindsided when asked about the issue. Thomas, along with his folks from Ducks Unlimited and Fish and Wildlife, met with DNR officials and explained what happened. DNR understood, and in the end no fines were issued, Thomas said.

Fishing was relaxation, a way to get his mind off things, including in the days before his wedding and before the draft, Gryzwa said.

It also was a cause.

In 2007, Wisconsin wildlife officials detected viral hemorrhagic septicemia — VHS — virus. Officials deemed it "a significant threat" to the fishing industry. The virus had been around since the 1930s and made its way to the West Coast of the United States in the 1980s. From there, it hit the Great Lakes. While no threat to humans, it was deadly to a variety of fish, including muskie, trout and bass. As part of a media-awareness campaign, Wisconsin DNR posted warnings at boat landings — don't move fish, clean boats or drain live wells. Statewide television and radio ads featured celebrities including Thomas, urging the rules to be followed.

That love of fishing continues. A now classic video, just more than a minute long, shows Thomas in a boat with his 9-year-old daughter Logan fishing. Excitedly, she catches what turns out to be a large muskellunge. The loudest screams weren't from Logan, though. They were from Thomas, roaring over happiness for his daughter.

Steve Johnson, Thomas' childhood pal, also has seen Thomas' love of nature.

"We go out to his farm, and we'd be kind of poking around on a gator (all-terrain utility vehicle). And we were driving around and all Joe's talking about are his trees. I mean, we're like, 'What a beautiful property, holy cow, this is crazy.' And Joe's saying, 'Over here we have a black walnut. And this is a this, and this is a that and I'm thinking if anybody cares less about the types of trees that are on this farm, it's me. And he's, 'Oh, man, these are just beautiful in the spring and beautiful in the fall.' His obsession with trees and nature far exceeds mine."

The outdoors life continues for Thomas, but his competitive side still has an outlet or two.

In 2020, a slimmed-down Thomas competed in several season-2 episodes of "The Titan Games," an NBC show featuring a gladiator-style obstacle course that tested competitors' strength and endurance while requiring quickness to maneuver through a route.

"This is the most insane athletic competition ever devised," host Dwayne "The Rock" Johnson announced, with an over-the-top marketing wail.

Thomas forged through the "Mount Olympus" course, pushing obstacles, turning levers to drop bridges, crawling in a cage and tugging a giant 300-pound ball.

You think football announcers become animated? Hyperbole was thick with the play-by-play here. "Icons in their world coming together to compete in this incredible challenge!" an announcer excitedly describes.

For the 2019 season, Thomas joined NFL Network's on-location pregame and postgame shows for Thursday Night Football. He also was part of the network's coverage for the Super Bowl, the combine, the draft and other programs. In early 2022, Thomas' name surfaced as a potential replacement for Browns radio analyst Doug Dieken, who had announced his retirement.

"Yeah, I enjoy doing broadcast," he said. "Right now I'm hoping to just kind of do enough to stay relevant so that maybe when the kids are old and go away, and I have a little more time, I'll be able to maybe do a little bit more of that."

Mike Lucas, who transitioned from his job as a sportswriter with the Capital Times to broadcast and communication roles with the University of Wisconsin, covered Thomas throughout his college days. "I've been doing this for over 50 years, covering Wisconsin football. And I've watched his growth. He's always been sharp. He's become just far more outgoing after this pro experience. And it's a matter of Joe recognizing what he needed to do to be successful after football, and that was to attack the television medium, which is what he has done. He has been more expressive. I think he really enjoys the analytical part of the game itself, which lends itself to the role that he's playing in the booth or even in the studio."

After he retired, the honors kept coming. He became the 14th player from the University of Wisconsin elected to the College Football Hall of Fame, in 2019. The same year, his high school alma mater inducted him into its Hall of Fame. Then, in 2020, Elmbrook School Board approved the naming of the Brookfield Central athletic field after Kenny Harrison and Thomas. Harrison, a 1983 Central graduate, had won a gold medal in the triple jump in the 1996 Olympics in Atlanta. In 2022, Thomas was inducted into the Browns Legends program, which recognizes the team's all-time greats.

And the pinnacle of any NFL player's career came in 2023 when, in his first year of eligibility, Thomas was elected to the Hall of Fame.

The definition of "beloved" athletes or sports figures is an interesting one. Deciding who are beloved Cleveland athletes would be a rich pool to swim in — and worthy of bar arguments.

What does it mean to be beloved? It transcends just making that great catch, scoring the winning run, or hauling in a playoff touchdown. It is earned, an organic affinity that is as real to fans as the player's accomplishments on a field or court. It's intangible — there is no set-in-stone definition.

First, it wouldn't be the greatest necessarily, though greatness would obviously figure into it.

Baseball player Ray Chapman and boxer Johnny Kilbane are early great and beloved athletes who represented Cleveland. The former was tragically cut down in his prime while the boxer — a Cleveland native — was a dynastic champion.

Bernie Kosar was a Northeast Ohio guy who played for the Browns and still remains popular at signings and appearances. He owns a Super Bowl ring — though not with Cleveland.

Mark Price fit a bit of an underdog role, a 6-foot point guard who played for the Cavaliers. But he doesn't live here.

Terry Francona led the Cleveland Indians to a World Series appearance in 2016 and has been in Cleveland longer than any team he has managed. Living downtown and being captured on his scooter motoring the few blocks to and from the ballpark doesn't hurt his image.

But off-field demeanor can tarnish a reputation and overshadow on-field accomplishments. Any list is debatable, to be sure.

Jim Brown arguably can be called the greatest running back of all time, though his past will forever be linked to his treatment of women, a pattern of abuse.

Jim Thome was loved for his homers in Cleveland, though many fans remain bitter over Thome leaving for Philadelphia.*

Omar Vizquel entertained fans with his acrobatic infield work with the Indians, though sexual misconduct allegations clearly tipped the scales against him when it comes to potential Hall of Fame inclusion.

LeBron James will go down undoubtedly as one of the greatest

---

* The stark contrast to how Northeast Ohio fans feel about Thome was seen after he spoke at a dinner in 2022 — a decade after he retired. Attendees filled a ballroom to hear Thome and his wife speak. But afterward, emails from fans with long memories barraged reporter Marc Bona, who had covered the event. Fans remained upset because Thome had left Cleveland for Philadelphia after the 2002 season — *20 years earlier*. Long memories Clevelanders have.

NBA players, and being a kid from Akron doesn't hurt. Leading the Cavaliers to a championship in 2016 warms Clevelanders' hearts, as does his commitment to education for local youngsters. But on July 8, 2010, the decision he made and announced on national television to leave Cleveland was akin to a slap that still stings.

Rocky Colavito has to be considered in this rarefied air. A home-run hitter who endeared himself to fans, he left because of a notorious trade that doesn't just linger but remains entrenched like a scar from an old wound. Half a century after last donning a baseball uniform, Colavito could still draw crowds for the rare book signing or statue unveiling (his likeness graces Tony Brush Park in Cleveland's Little Italy). Hundreds of people crammed into the tiny park for his statue ceremony in 2021, on Colavito's 88th birthday.

Filmmaker Andy Billman, an Elyria native and former ESPN producer, offers up the Indians' Kenny Lofton ("To me he is the face of the '90s teams"), the Browns' Clay Matthews Jr. ("I know some will debate"), the Cavaliers' Price, Larry Nance and Austin Carr; Kosar ("amazing his star power in this town"), the Guardians' Jose Ramirez ("by the time he's done") and Paul Brown. The latter, of course, is the football team's namesake and pioneer in the sport who invented and promoted many parts of the game that remain in use, from the draw play to the practice squad.

Carr has remained prominent in the media because of his longtime analyst role for Cavs games. Larry Doby is remembered fondly, and more accepted now than he was when he played. Andre Thornton, Sandy Alomar? Both had very good careers and remain well-liked by fans.

It's fair to put Thomas on the list of beloved Cleveland athletes.

Why an athlete is — or becomes — great involves multiple variables. Heart, dedication, or a will to win figure into it. Hard work is the behind-the-scenes sweat and hours in a weight room or miles logged running, arduous exercises done when no cameras are around.

In Thomas' case, there might be another explanation: Bone density.

Athletes of all sports are measured in so many ways, but football players — especially at the combine — undergo a series of scrutinized tests that calculate all things physical. Bone density is one of them.

"One time," his mother Sally said, "he told me he was in some pileup, and he said, 'Mom, if my legs weren't as tough, my bones as thick, I know I would have broken something.'"

DXA — dual-energy X-ray absorption — measures fat, lean and bone mass, and density. The machine used to measure bone density is called a DEXA scan, Thomas explained, with 1 as a baseline representing normal bone density. A nutritionist who was running the scans told Thomas of the thousands of athletes she'd tested in college and professional sports, the most dense bone reading she ever recorded was a 3.0.

"And I was a 5.0. That was almost twice as dense as the most dense bones that she's ever tested. And my wife would probably say, 'That makes perfect sense; your brain is just as dense.'"

Low-hanging fruit joke aside, Thomas said it explains a few things. A sports scientist told him the density measurement is akin to building a house. If you want to go up 10 stories, you have to make it with steel, that wood is simply not strong enough. And if you want to be able to handle a lot of muscle and weight, "you've got to have really dense bones to be able to handle that. Otherwise, your skeletal system just won't be able to produce force, right? But you can produce a lot of force when you're a very rigid structure on the inside. So that explains a lot. You know, I was always a powerful person, but I was not always somebody who maybe was the strongest in the weight room. And I never broke a bone in 20 years or whatever of football and more than that, in other sports. Not a finger, not an arm, not a leg. If anything, I have bone spurs from bone growth around my tendons. I had the opposite; I need less bone."

Bone density came naturally. Other physiological aspects were achieved through smart work. Take the case of "TV arms."

Thomas' former Browns teammate Evan Moore says during the

season it was normal throughout the league after an easy practice on Fridays for players to go into the weight room. Strength coaches would have a circuit set up strictly for biceps. It took on the nickname of "TV arms," so guys can work on their arms on Friday to look good on television on Sunday. Strength coaches don't want to tax players' legs before a game, Moore said.

One day Moore was working out when Thomas walked in. "One of the younger guys yells, 'Hey Joe, you want to do some TV arms with us?' And Joe just starts busting up, laughing. He says, 'You guys are such idiots. I'm heading over to do TV stretching. This is what keeps me on television — stretching.' And for a guy who played 10,363 snaps in a row, how about that. And he spent 45 minutes stretching after a Friday practice. Which again, that's Joe. He couldn't care less what looks good, what is perceived to be right — all that BS. He doesn't care about it. He was the guy who was always going to find the thing that was going to help him be more productive, even if it wasn't enjoyable."

Thanks in part to the era when he played, Thomas remains in the public eye, and has done so by maintaining a lifestyle devoid of controversy. Occasional Twitter opinions are witty, sometimes polarizing in a minor way, but never offensive. Like many athletes, Thomas hasn't shied from social media, using it as a forum to express opinions and shape his message. He teamed with former teammate Andrew Hawkins for a podcast, The ThomaHawk Show. Milwaukee Journal Sentinel's JR Radcliffe, writing about the podcast, wrote in 2017 that Thomas' "personality has been given even more time to shine through on social media. His mix of advocacy and self-deprecating humor showcases his thoughtfulness and suggests he's going to have a long and fruitful career after he plays."

Thomas' reputation doesn't just lie with serious honors. He has had not one but seven bobbleheads in his likeness: One is as a Wisconsin Badger, another shows him in a Lake Erie Monsters hockey uniform, in addition to several in Browns uniforms. But his off-the-field activities, ventures and business sense goes beyond the nodding figures found on office desks and bookcases.

Self-admittedly frugal, Thomas does say, "I'm probably less frugal with my wife and my kids now, but I certainly was very frugal. I think that's just my Midwest background. My mom would probably say it's my German background, but I don't know if that has anything to do with it. But yeah, definitely appreciate the value of a dollar."

There's a famous story about Thomas as a college senior, sharing a house with his pals. As the story goes, Ben Strickland — Thomas' close friend from high school and college — had underpaid a cable bill by a few dollars. Thomas left a note on his door for the remaining amount. It was just a few dollars.

"Well, you know, a deal's a deal," Thomas recalled years later. "We all agreed to split the cable bill. And just because I got drafted in the NFL doesn't mean that those guys don't have to pay their fair share."

The frugality applies to himself. In college, Thomas wore 72. The Badgers assigned it to him. Certain jerseys are given to players they have high hopes for, to live up to the pressure of the jersey wearer's previous owner—in this case, Al Johnson, a solid lineman who went on to play several years in the NFL. When Thomas got to the NFL, Ryan Tucker wore 72.* As is tradition, players who want to switch jerseys have a price to pay — literally. But Thomas said, he wasn't about to spend thousands of dollars on the jersey.

In fairness, it's not just frugality driving Thomas but a business sense.

Ted Kellner, a Wisconsin businessman and philanthropist, met Thomas through former Wisconsin football coach Barry Alvarez. Kellner worked with Wisconsin athletes through a program that helped educate them on financial principles, real-estate business and money management.

"I give them a book or two to read. But if I gave Joe a book on Thursday, he'd call me on Tuesday and say, 'You got any more books?' I think I gave him two more books on Tuesday. And he

---

* Another season and Thomas might have had a shot at his old number. Tucker played 12 years in the NFL, but 2008 — Thomas' second in the league—was his last.

called me in two weeks asking if I had any more books. I have, you know, some kids who never read the books. But I think in three weeks, Joe had read three or four books. He had an intense interest in the stock market and investing in real estate."

Kellner and Thomas have stayed in touch, and both work with the university on its NIL — Name, Image and Likeness — initiative, the Varsity Collective.

Name, Image and Likeness is a recent shift in collegiate athletics to allow student-athletes to receive compensation for the use of their personal NIL. In the past, schools reaped the benefit of potential marketing deals regarding their athletes, but the change under NCAA regulations now allows them more flexibility when it comes to earning power. The University of Wisconsin's Varsity Collective aims to help student-athletes navigate their NIL through education, support and partnerships.

Thomas is part of the consortium of those helping athletes. He and his wife, Annie, are doing a Varsity Collective-sponsored podcast with current and former players to get the word out.

NIL wasn't around when Thomas was playing. Endorsements became an option during his professional career. But offensive linemen aren't going to become wealthy off promotions for companies or products. Most players do not have a stable of multiple endorsements, like Peyton Manning, who seems to be on every other television commercial. Unlike Aaron Rodgers or Patrick Mahomes, most don't land deals that bring in a lot of money while adding to their media visibility. And fewer still can be in a position like LeBron James, whose star power has led not only to endorsements but often pieces of companies or multiple avenues of media outreach for exposure and revenue. But offensive linemen? Most don't get even the kind of exposure that players like Joel Bitonio and Jack Conklin receive, as they tout a Cleveland-area car company with a poor man's rap and some stilted dance moves.

"One of the arguments that I've made about NIL," Thomas said, "all these people who think all of a sudden there's going to be just a windfall of money for college athletes, regardless of the position.

Look, I was probably, out of anybody on the team in any given year, the person who had the most endorsements. Not that I was a big name. And part of that was because we just didn't have a ton of big names. But I mean, I still only had just a couple. So it's not like it was tons of money. I mean, of course, if you're Gronkowski or Brady or Manning, big names like Mahomes, course, they've got tons of endorsements. But outside of those top-20-jersey-seller type guys, it's really not all that much available. I mean, you can hustle and you can do a few things, but it's not crazy."

His big deal was with Under Armour, the athletic apparel brand. He also promoted the National Dairy Council and Universal Windows Direct. And after he retired, he worked with Great Lakes Brewing Co., the first craft brewery in Ohio. Thomas had been neighbors with Bill Boor, the former chief executive of Great Lakes, when he moved to Northeast Ohio in 2007. The two talked beer, and an idea took root. But it remained just that — an idea, since current players are restricted from alcohol and tobacco promotion.

But the idea fermented. Thomas showed a willingness to soak up knowledge — just as Kellner described about working with Thomas the business student. Thomas visited the brewery in June 2018 and immersed himself in the comprehension of brewing. In the end, the brewery keeps coming out with 73 Kolsch, a quaffable beer.

The beer isn't the only food or beverage Thomas would be associated with. Not long before the deal with the brewery, the Akron RubberDucks, Cleveland's Class AA baseball team, unveiled a special menu item in his honor: A sandwich called "Thanks, Joe!"

The hoagie-roll sandwich held two butterfly-sliced bratwursts from Cleveland-based Five Star Brand. The brats were smothered in craft-beer cheese, onions and peppers. Cost: $10.

"Thanks, Joe!" is now a bit ironic because, while it was a hearty, tasty, two-hands-required sandwich, it is doubtful it would fall into a daily diet for Thomas, who maintains a keen focus on nutrition and grows vegetables on his farm.

So in addition to the snap streak and Pro Bowl appearances, Thomas had bobbleheads, beer and a brat sandwich in his honor.

Fame has been an interesting dynamic, said Thomas, who is recognized in Madison but definitely not as "a celebrity-type thing. I don't have a lot of people who come up and ask for autographs or pictures or anything like that. But that's definitely the case in Cleveland."

Thomas' reputation leans toward humility rather than someone who has an outward bravado. Had he ever scored a touchdown, it's hard to picture him dancing around in the end zone, pantomiming and taunting. Maybe a ball slam, then trot off the field. But make no mistake: Every player in the NFL has a level of confidence that can range from extroverted, showy and camera-mugging outbursts to a more latent confidence. Thomas was in the latter group.

As his high school teammate Adam Dahlke said: "He was just humble. It's funny, because, when you hear him talk on TV, really nothing's changed."

Evan Moore, who played with Thomas on the Browns from 2009 to 2011, recounts a classic story of being in the cafeteria with Thomas once during training camp in 2010:

> Joe Thomas had already been in the league three years, and then Joe Haden rolls in as the No. 1 pick for the Browns that year. As nice of a guy as Joe Thomas is, and as easy as he is to talk to, as gracious as he is, well, you can't be that good and that dominant at your craft—especially when it involves playing football—without having a confident edge to you. It's impossible to accomplish what he's accomplished without having just a trace of "I'm the shit" to you. Joe does a good job of not letting it come out very often, but you know it's there. You can't accomplish what he accomplished without doing it.
>
> So we're in the cafeteria, middle of training camp. It's a lunch after practice or something like that. I'm sitting next to Joe Thomas with one or two other guys at the table, just hanging out, talking. And Joe Haden walks up and sits down. He's a rookie; none of us really knew him very well yet. (Now, of course, everyone loves Joe Haden; he was a great teammate.)

"What's up guys?" Haden says.

Joe Thomas says, "What's up, Joe? How's it going?"

"Shoot, man, I'm just trying to be like you," Joe Haden responds, which is sort of an awkward way of responding when you don't know what else to say. A lot of guys do it.

Joe Thomas starts belly laughing. We can all hear it. And he says, "Oh, my gosh, holy shit. Well, you have a fucking *loonnng* way to go if that's the case!"

All of us sat there looking at each other, like, "Did he really just say that?"

And Joe Haden sat there and kind of nodded, like he agreed. And he looked down and kept eating his food.

Thomas has always maintained a sense of humor. In a video to promote the 2023 Greater Cleveland Sports Awards, which he had just been named to host, he poked fun at the mustache he had grown, calling it a "cookie duster." On air, wearing a bright orange shirt in a postgame analysis, he remarked to his broadcast partner they had to get going to return their shirts to the local prison. At a 2017 Taste of the Browns fundraiser for the Greater Cleveland Food Bank, Thomas was asked what he liked to eat as a kid. Without missing a beat, he said: "Growing up I drank a lot of beer when I was a child and ate cheese curds. So without those two staples I wouldn't be the size I am today."

Thomas definitely had a good time Nov. 7, 2010. That Sunday, the Browns, coming off a bye week, hosted the New England Patriots and Tom Brady. With no love lost for coach Bill Belichick, fans saw Cleveland come out on top, 34-14. It was one of only two regular-season losses for the Patriots that season. Peyton Hillis ran for a career-best 184 yards. As Belichick came across the field to congratulate Browns coach Eric Mangini, Thomas chest-bumped his own offensive coordinator, Brian Daboll. Daboll is no small guy, but Thomas was bigger, almost a decade younger and in pads. As Moore puts it, Thomas "de-cleated" the coach. The Browns would go 5-11 that season, but a win over the Brady Patriots and a monumental chest bump — well, that's priceless. In an ironic connection, on Feb. 9, 2023, Thomas was elected to the Hall of Fame, and Daboll was elected 2022 Associated Press NFL Coach of the Year.

Thomas also had a good time with a pregame promotional routine the Browns started in 2022. A celebrity "Dawg Pound Captain" comes out of the tunnel, ramps up the crowd, and opens a case that contains a guitar with the opponent's colors. He then smashes it as smoke spews and the crowd goes wild. Thomas, of course, who is not shy from letting his inner ham come out, ate it up. He implored the crowd to cheer, slid on protective goggles, and then — with a two-handed windup — smashed the guitar with "Jets" on it to the crowd's delight. The guitar splintered, pieces flying. On this day, though, Thomas didn't have enough mojo. The Jets won, 31-30.

Thomas played in 10 Pro Bowls, from his rookie year — 2007 — through 2016. To put that in perspective, look at his position in the Hall of Fame: Only six Hall of Fame offensive linemen have played in more consecutive Pro Bowls — Bruce Matthews (14), Jim Otto (12), Will Shields (12), Randall McDaniel (12), Anthony Muñoz (11) and Jonathan Ogden (11).

Through 2022, the Hall of Fame has 362 members. Of those, 51 are modern-era linemen. Of those 51, 12 were first ballot: Larry Allen, Forrest Gregg, John Hannah, Walter Jones, Jim Langer, Matthews, Muñoz, Ogden, Otto, Jim Parker, Jackie Slater and Gene Upshaw.

But it's more than the statistics where Thomas shines. Moore was there, and saw Thomas day in and day out, enduring losses but also the ingrained culture around him.

"You could say that a left tackle being on an island, just doing his job, maybe it's easier for him to be successful, despite all the lack of success of an organization, whereas you know, receivers, tight ends, they have to rely on a quarterback and all that stuff. I call BS on that," Moore said. "I think no matter what position you play, to be able to rise above the muck, and to be able to do what Joe did is just incredible."

What Moore witnessed day in and day out included a turnstile of quarterbacks. That has to wear on players.

"Losing is like an infection, and it spreads throughout a locker room and spreads throughout an organization to where the standard of what people expect for everybody lowers because everyone is, 'We're just a bunch of losers,' more or less, like we're all used to losing and we all make excuses. And for Joe to just continue to rise above that and ignore all that, for that many years — that alone to me is more impressive than if he had played 10,300 snaps for a good team. It's almost more impressive that he's done what he's done, despite all the losing. Some people might say, 'Joe Thomas, you know, Hall of Famer? How many playoff games has that guy been to?'

"For Joe to be able to just put his head down — and I'm not saying it wasn't hard for him. I know from talking to him a bunch there were moments where it was hard, he wanted to quit it was so hard. But for him to rise above that the way he did and to see his approach every single day, despite all this just terrible decision making, bad attitude, losing culture, all that just surrounded him every day. And he never let it affect him. I just think that's amazing."

Moore was just one of the many teammates who Thomas lined up alongside — from youth sports to high school, from college ball to the NFL. Players hit a level of greatness to make it that far, but in Thomas, Moore saw something else. It went beyond the preparation and the toughness. There was a sense of pride he saw in his friend.

"When I look at Joe in his stance, and watch Joe kick-step as an offensive lineman or move up the field and drive-block somebody in the run game, you realize real quickly that Joe was the 1 percent of the 1 percent of the 1 percent."

THE HALL OF FAME
(IN JOE'S WORDS)

"Something I will remember until the day I die."

In my very first interview with the Cleveland media I told them that my goal was to make the Pro Football Hall of Fame. Looking back, it was a pretty bold claim for a guy who had never played a snap in the NFL, but shouldn't everyone aspire to be the best?

You can't have goals that are less than perfection. I truly believe that. I try to do everything to perfection in my life, and I'm not satisfied until it happens. That's the way I live my life. That's the way I was raised.

So I laid out my career goals. First be a starter, then be a good reliable starter, then make the Pro Bowl, and if you do that enough times you give yourself the chance to reach your dream of making the Hall of Fame. It was a step-by-step process for me, but I knew I had to take it one day at a time. No one makes the Hall of Fame overnight. You get there by having a good day today, then again tomorrow and just continuing to get better every day.

Looking back, by focusing on each day, I was able to put together a football resume that I am proud of. I ended up making 10 Pro Bowls and being named to the NFL All-Pro team eight times. But the thing I was most proud of was the snap streak of 10,363 straight plays.

I always had a motto in my head: "Count on me." When times get tough, I wanted people to know they could count on me. My parents did a great job of just ingraining that in my head growing up. That was always a part of my character, my identity. I wanted my coaches, teammates and fans to know that they could count on me. That's why that snap streak was so special to me. For 10,363 plays, which ended up being every play of my career, I can hang my hat knowing that I gave everything I had and that everyone could count on me.

They say the days crawl by, but the years fly by. That's exactly how it felt for me after my retirement following the 2017 season. The only requirement the Pro Football Hall of Fame has for a player or coach is that they must have been retired at least five years before they can be considered. It didn't feel like it had been five years, but all of a sudden people started talking about the Pro Football Hall Fame Class of 2023.

The Hall of Fame announced a list of 129 nominees in September 2022. The list was trimmed to 28 semifinalists in November and then to 15 finalists in January. I was lucky enough to be on that list of finalists. The final list of five players selected for induction in Canton, Ohio, was going to be announced at the NFL awards show called NFL Honors, in February right before the Super Bowl.

The Hall of Fame's 49-person selection committee was going to decide my fate. The committee consists of one media representative from each pro football city and other media members who are heavily involved in professional football. Every finalist is reviewed and must receive approval from at least 80 percent of the committee to be elected.

Starting in 2016, the committee would hold a secret vote and all the finalists would be in a hotel room awaiting a knock on the door from David Baker, then the president of the Hall of Fame. It was a made-for-TV moment dubbed "The Knock." Players would wait in their room with friends and family. It was life-changing news that made your favorite gridiron giants weep. Those selected then were rushed to the NFL Honors show, announced to the world and later enshrined in the hall. Those who did not get in received a phone call saying better luck next year.

The COVID-19 pandemic in 2020, along with the negative feelings related to the guys who got the "better luck next year" call, led to a new and better way to do things. Everything wasn't done during a span of hours anymore. The committee voted long before NFL Honors and inductees were surprised with 'The Knock" by members of the Hall of Fame to share the life-altering news. These happened at different locations across the country, but everything was still kept a secret until the NFL Honors show.

I assumed that if I made it then the surprise knock would come in the week prior to the show. You are dealing with 49 media members, countless members of the Hall as well as inductees and their families. That's a lot of people to try to keep a secret so I thought they would keep that timing as tight as they could so news didn't leak.

It was a little surreal thinking that I was so close to being voted in. More than 15 years ago as a rookie I boldly declared my goals of making the Pro Football Hall of Fame to the media. It was a big goal, but I was glad I had big dreams.

It was about a month before the NFL Honors show, and the Hall of Fame was the furthest thing from my mind. We had recently returned from a family vacation in Mexico. It was a Friday afternoon, and the kids were all home from school. We had plans to go out with our neighbors that evening. My wife, Annie, said that we needed to have a family meeting. Usually that means the kids aren't listening to her and she needs dad to come help set the kids straight.

I was almost ready for our evening out with the neighbors, but I was just in a shirt and my underwear. Annie insisted that I put my pants on before the meeting. I didn't understand why, but she said we would be leaving as soon as the family meeting was over. Being the good husband I am, and knowing my wife is always right, I begrudgingly put on my pants.

I was in our kitchen and I heard the world's loudest knock on the door. At first, I thought it was the neighbor kids coming over to play with my kids. Logan, Camryn, Jack and Reese ran to the door thinking that they had company, but it was not the neighbor kids.

My daughter, Camryn, ran back into the kitchen and said, "It's a man in a jacket and coat." I thought maybe it was a door-to-door salesman, someone looking to sell us insurance or pest control.

The next thing I knew, Jack came flying into the kitchen, jumping up and down like a jackrabbit yelling, "We made it Dad, we made it!"

It took me a few seconds to register that the loud banging on the door was "The Knock." I was caught completely off guard. I was just not expecting it to happen that soon, that far out from the announcement. I was also grateful I had pants on.

The kids were all going crazy as I walked toward the door. I opened it to find former Seattle Seahawks Hall of Fame tackle Walter Jones standing on my doorstep in his gold jacket with about 15 people with cameras and boom microphones.

He said, "Welcome to the Hall of Fame," and I asked if I could give him a hug. It all hit me. I was emotionally knocked off my feet. I started crying. I was sure I wasn't going to be emotional, but it just caught me so much off guard with the way they did it. With my kids being there and my son being the first to yell, "We made it." Being able to see my all my kids' pure excitement and joy. And also with it being big Walter Jones, it was just so perfect. It is something I will remember until the day I die. The moment was just magical.

When I was young and trying to learn the tackle position, I watched Walter Jones. He is one of the best to ever do it. I idolized him. I couldn't believe that he was the one to welcome me home to Canton. There he was standing on my front porch. Now keep in mind, this is Wisconsin in January and the wind chill was about 10 below zero that day. Everyone just stood there as I was an emotional mess. I was eventually able to compose myself and everyone just kept staring at me. I didn't know it, but they were all just waiting on me to ask them to come inside the house. I had no idea. I had never done this before. Finally, as they continued to stand there freezing, I asked half joking, "So do you guys come inside now, or do you just leave?"

My wife was the only person in my family who was in on the surprise. She knew she couldn't trust the kids to keep it a secret. To help show that I wasn't prepared, once everyone got inside and warm, we went to do a celebration champagne toast and all we had in the house was a cheap $12 bottle. It didn't matter, we popped it anyways and I was able to cheer with my wife and Walter Jones. We also got the kids ice cream. They tried to go crazy with extra chocolate syrup and mounds of sprinkles for the occasion, but Annie told them, "It's a celebration, not a free-for-all." Apparently, there is no off-switch for supermom mode.

I became the seventh offensive tackle in NFL history to be inducted in his first year of eligibility also known as a "first ballot" Hall of Famer. I am truly just in awe when I look at the list of other first-ballot tackles: Jackie Slater, Jim Parker, Forrest Gregg, Anthony Munoz, Jonathan Ogden and of course Walter Jones. The fact that I share the same honor with them is humbling. They were the best to ever do it and to be able to have just a little bit in common with them is something I don't take lightly.

It's not just an NFL tackle thing, either. It's a Cleveland Browns thing. To be the first player selected to the Hall of Fame since the team's return in 1999 is awesome. I am officially the 18th Cleveland Browns Hall of Famer, and I couldn't be prouder.

Growing up in Wisconsin I was a fan of Brett Favre and Reggie White. But those Packer fans kind of have to share those Hall of Fame guys with other fan bases. Reggie White was an Eagle, a Packer and a Panther. Favre was a Falcon, Packer, Jet and Viking. I am so honored that I can be a Hall of Famer that Browns fans can say, "He played his whole career with us." Browns fans have endured some really tough times, but those fans are so loyal and passionate. Being able to share this with them is really special to me.

Even though "The Knock" came about a month in advance of NFL Honors, we were able to keep everything a secret until then. When that time finally came, we brought the whole family for the official announcement because we wanted to make sure we were making memories alongside them. During NFL Honors, they brought the Pro Football Hall of Fame Class of 2023 out on stage, and I was there waving to the crowd. It was a great moment because I could now officially share it with everyone else.

The next day, they had us for the Merlin Olsen Luncheon. They announced us as Hall of Famers, and we had to walk up on the stage in front of about 70 other Hall of Famers all in their gold jackets. I looked around and saw the absolute legends of the game, guys who I cheered for, standing up and clapping for me. I remember my knees just crumbling and going weak. It is one of many overwhelming emotional moments that I had that weekend. I also got to meet some of my heroes growing up. LeRoy Butler from the Packers, someone I admired as a kid, came and told me that he was happy that I made the Hall of Fame. I saw Barry Sanders, Joe Namath, Orlando Pace, and I got to take photos with them. A part of me was waiting for security to come and kick me out. It was really awesome having that opportunity to just spend time with the greats who came before you. I just couldn't believe that I get to wear the same jacket and be a part of the same club as those legends.

Another time when things really hit me was "Sizing Saturday." They measure the Hall of Famers for rings, gold jackets and their bust sculpture. I got to sit with a world-famous sculptor as he took photos and my measurements. I asked him if he could make my nose and ears a little smaller after he told me that they were definitely some of the biggest that he has ever measured. I don't think he is going to take my suggestion, but the fact that there will be a bust of my face is just surreal.

I think back to what my son Jack said when we realized what was going on during "The Knock." It was so appropriate that he said, "We made it," because that's what it took. It was always about we, not me. The Hall of Fame is certainly a celebration of one person's career, but it's more so a celebration of every person who has touched that person's life.

I look at it kind of like a string of 1,000 dominos. Yes, I was able to reach the highest honor that a football player can achieve, but every coach, parent, teammate, teacher, family member and mentor along the way represented one of those dominos. If you take just one of those dominos away, then maybe my story is different. I am so grateful for everyone who helped me on this path. I wouldn't have made it without them.

ACKNOWLEDGMENTS

So many people helped directly and indirectly in this project.

Those who knew, coached, played with, or competed against Joe Thomas at various levels of his life were helpful and willing to go down memory lane: Mark Adams, Bob Berghaus, Bret Bielema, Joel Bitonio, Ronn Blaha, Adam Ciborowski, Adam Dahlke, John Greco, Jeff Gryzwa, Nick Hamel, Brandon Houle, Steve Johnson, Ted Kellner, Mike Lucas, Alex Mack, Steve Marcelle, Jamie Meulemans, Evan Moore, Joel Nellis, Scott Nelson, Mitchell Schwartz, John Stocco and Ben Strickland.

The Milwaukee-area media did a solid job of covering Joe Thomas in college, with two bylines in particular coming up repeatedly: Mike Lucas of The Capital Times and the late Tom Mulhern of the Wisconsin State Journal. Their coverage was outstanding.

Others guided, helping with an interview, fact checking or context.

Former La Crosse Tribune reporter Anne Aldrich-Abraham, who covered the tragic Luke Homan case so thoroughly and with dignity, spoke about the aftermath of the young man's death. My friend and author Chris Lamb was my editor in college, and in a way still is: He continues to offer great advice. Brett Moore of the University of Illinois was so responsive to my queries. On each of my books, I have received invaluable advice from my colleague Bob Higgs, a reporter and lawyer. Chris Quinn, vice president of content for Advance Local, was generous with use of photos. Skip Hall added his usual deft copy editing touch.

Andrew Gribble, Pat Murphy and Mike Fielder provided valuable feedback and suggestions along the way.

Don Kurth and Yvette Cunningham from the athletic department at Brookfield Central High School rolled out the red — or should I say royal blue, silver and white — carpet. Joe's parents, Sally and Eric Thomas, welcomed me into their home minutes after they had returned from a trip. They graciously answered my fact-checking questions while reminiscing about their son.

Publisher David Gray made great suggestions along the way, and agent Anne Devlin has been with me on this project.

Others answering random fact-checking queries: Eric Schumacher-Rasmussen, Jeff Potrykus, Azenett Cornejo, Adam Liberman, Kevin Seitzer, Mike Hogan, the Pro Football Hall of Fame's Jon Kendle, Joseph Ricciotti of the National Oceanic and Atmospheric Administration and Brett Gruetzmacher of Brookfield Central High School.

It's proof writing a book is both a solitary and communal endeavor. Many thanks to all.

BIBLIOGRAPHY

BOOKS

Doster, Rob, editor. "Game Day: Wisconsin Football," Chicago Triumph Books, 2007.

Gault, William Campbell. "Mr. Fullback." New York: E.P. Dutton & Co., 1953.

Ramstack, Thomas. "Images of America: Brookfield and Elm Grove," Mt. Pleasant, S.C.: Arcadia Publishing, 2009.

Schlichenmeyer, Terri and Mark Meier. "The Handy Wisconsin Answer Book," Detroit: Visible Ink Press, 2019.

Windhorst, Brian. "LeBron Inc.: The Making of a Billion Dollar Athlete," New York: Grand Central Publishing, 2019.

NEWSPAPERS AND RELATED MEDIA

Associated Press
Atlanta Journal-Constitution
Barron News-Shield
The Capital Times, Madison
Columbus Dispatch
Daily Citizen, Beaver Dam
Daily Tribune, Wisconsin Rapids
Green Bay Press-Gazette
The Journal Times, Racine
Kenosha News
La Crosse Tribune
Leader-Telegram, Eau Claire
Milwaukee Journal Sentinel

The Plain Dealer, Cleveland
Portage Daily Register
The Post Crescent, Appleton
The Reporter, Fond du Lac
Republican Eagle, Cannon Falls, Minnesota
The Sheboygan Press
Stevens Point Journal
USA Today
The Washington Post
Wausau Daily Herald, Wausau
Wisconsin State Journal, Madison

PERSONAL INTERVIEWS

Mark Adams
Anne Aldrich-Abraham
Bob Berghaus
Bret Bielema
Joel Bitonio
Ronn Blaha
Adam Ciborowski
Adam Dahlke
John Greco

Jeff Gryzwa
Nick Hamel
Brandon Houle
Steve Johnson
Ted Kellner
Mike Lucas
Alec Mack
Steve Marcelle
Jamie Meulemans

Evan Moore
Joel Nellis
Scott Nelson
Mitchell Schwartz
John Stocco
Ben Strickland
Eric Thomas
Joe Thomas
Sally Thomas

WEBSITES

247sports.com

afca.com

ametsoc.org

andscape.com

audacy.com (Ken Carmen with
    Anthony Lima podcast)

blackheartgoldpants.com

buccaneers.com

clevelandbrowns.com

flashresults.com

footballreference.com

grantland.com

greatbusinessschools.org

kidshealth.org

madison.com

mountsinai.org

nfl.com

onthisday.com

sports-reference.com

uwbadgers.com

worldathletics.org

wunderground.com

ABOUT THE AUTHORS

Marc Bona is a features writer for cleveland.com who previously worked in assorted editing roles for The Plain Dealer in Cleveland; The Post-Tribune in Gary, Indiana; The Times Union in Albany, New York; The Detroit News; San Antonio Light and The Dallas Morning News. Winner of numerous Cleveland Press Club writing awards, he has written three previous books. A football-based novel, "The Game Changer," was published in 2018. "Hidden History of Cleveland Sports" and "The Reason We Play" both came out in 2021. A graduate of the University of Iowa, he lives in Akron with his wife, Lynne Sherwin, and their rescue pup, Addie. He can be reached at mbona30@neo.rr.com.

Dan Murphy is director of football communications for the Cleveland Browns. Initially joining the Browns as an intern in 2008, Murphy currently leads the day-to-day communications and media operations efforts. He oversees all player interviews, helps craft messaging for organizational spokespersons and directs production and dissemination of the team's football information (media guide, game notes, press releases, statistics, history and records). He graduated with a bachelor's degree in communications from Hiram College and a master's degree in sport management from Eastern Michigan University. He lives in Mentor with his wife, Sara, and daughters Hayden and McKinley.

Other books of interest . . .

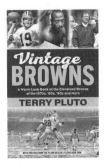

Vintage Browns
A Warm Look Back at the Cleveland Browns of the 1970s, '80s, '90s and More

Terry Pluto

Like a classic throwback jersey, this book recalls favorite players and moments from Cleveland Browns teams of the 1970s, '80s, '90s and more. Visit with Bernie Kosar, Ozzie Newsome, Brian Sipe, Marty Schottenheimer, Doug Dieken, Kevin Mack, Bill Belichik and others from days when the "Kardiac Kids" and the "Dawgs" ruled the old Stadium.

The Browns Blues
Two Decades of Utter Frustration: Why Everything Kept Going Wrong for the Cleveland Browns

Terry Pluto

How could things go so wrong for so long? From their return in 1999 through the winless 2017 season, the Cleveland Browns had the worst record in the NFL. And their fans had ulcers. Veteran sports columnist Terry Pluto explains two decades of front-office upheaval and frustrating football in this detailed, behind-the-scenes analysis.

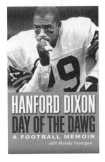

Day of the Dawg
A Football Memoir

Hanford Dixon, Randy Nyerges

The popular and outspoken NFL cornerback offers an inside look at the turbulent, exciting, and frustrating Cleveland Browns seasons of the 1980s. Dixon, a three-time Pro Bowler and co-inventor of the Dawg Pound, recalls both roller-coaster on-field action and a culture of drug use that permeated the NFL and led to the tragic death of a teammate.

More at **www.grayco.com**

Other books of interest . . .

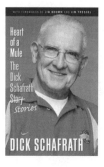

Heart of a Mule
Dick Schafrath

With forewords by Jim Brown and Jim Tressel

Browns and Ohio State legend Dick Schafrath shares a lifetime of stories: National football championships with the 1964 Cleveland Browns and the 1957 Ohio State Buckeyes. Four terms in the Ohio senate. He canoed across Lake Erie, met president, wrestled bears. Wild and wonderful, his tales reveal a dedication to hard work and a stubborn determination worthy of a mule.

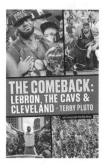

The Comeback: LeBron, the Cavs & Cleveland
How LeBron James Came Home and Brought a Championship to Cleveland

Terry Pluto

One of the greatest Cleveland sports stories ever! In this epic homecoming tale, LeBron James and the Cavaliers take fans on a roller coaster ride from despair to hope and, finally, to glory as the 2016 NBA champions. Terry Pluto tells how it all happened, with insightful analysis and behind-the-scenes details.

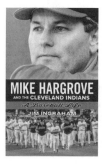

Mike Hargrove and the Cleveland Indians
A Baseball Life

Jim Ingraham

An inside, in-depth look a fascinating baseball life, from small-town sandlots to the World Series. Mike Hargrove played, managed and lived the game for four decades, with big moments both heartbreaking and heart-stopping. Rookie of the Year, All Star, a tragic accident, five consecutive division titles, the Game 7 loss, getting fired, and more.

More at **www.grayco.com**